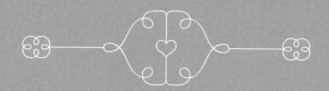

EAT LIKE AN ITALIAN

RECIPES FOR THE GOOD LIFE

CATHERINE FULVIO

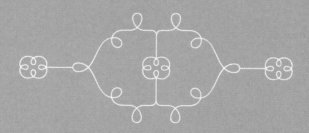

GILL & MACMILLAN

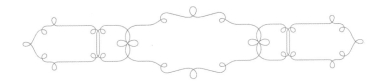

GILL & MACMILLAN
HUME AVENUE, PARK WEST
DUBLIN 12
WITH ASSOCIATED COMPANIES THROUGHOUT THE WORLD
www.gillmacmillanbooks.ie

ISBN: 978 07171 5467 8

DESIGNED BY www.grahamthew.com
PHOTOGRAPHY BY Harry Weir
INDEXED BY Cover to Cover
PRINTED BY Printer Trento, SRL, Italy

This book is typeset in Devinne Text.

The paper used in this book comes from the wood pulp of managed forests. For every tree felled, at least one tree is planted, thereby renewing natural resources.

A catalogue record for this book is available from the British Library.

54321

Items should be returned on or before the last date
shown below. Items not already requested by other
borrowers may be renewed in person, in writing or by
telephone. To renew, please quote the number on the
barcode label. To renew online a PIN is required.
This can be requested at your local library.
Renew online @ **www.dublincitypubliclibraries.ie**
Fines charged for overdue items will include postage
incurred in recovery. Damage to or loss of items will
be charged to the borrower.

**Leabharlanna Poiblí Chathair Bhaile Átha Cliath
Dublin City Public Libraries**

Drumcondra Branch Tel: 8377206

Baile Átha Cliath
Dublin City

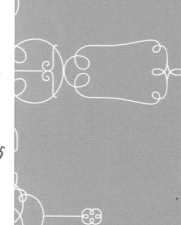

Date Due	Date Due	Date Due
17 OCT 2012		22 APR 2015
	02 MAR 2013	
19 NOV 2012		24 JUL 2015
10 DEC 2012	- 4 JUL 2013	07 OCT 2015
- 5 DEC 2013	25 JUL 2013	
	25 JAN 2014	09 DEC 2015
	25 FEB 2015	
		09 APR 2016
		3 AUG 2016
		24 JAN 2019

EAT LIKE AN ITALIAN
RECIPES FOR THE GOOD LIFE

 CONTENTS

FARRO AND TOMATO SALAD *48*
INSALATA DI FARRO E POMODORO

PARMESAN POLENTA CHIPS *49*
PATATINE DI POLENTA CON PARMIGIANO

FRUIT

SUMMER BERRIES WITH MAPLE ZABAGLIONE *56*
BACCHE ESTIVE CON ZABAGLIONE

FRESH FIG ICE CREAM *59*
GELATO DI FICHI

FRUIT GRANITA *60*
GRANITA DI FRUTTA

PLUM AND CHIANTI COMPOTE WITH GINGER *62*
PRUGNE AL CHIANTI E ZENZERO

ROASTED RHUBARB AND STRAWBERRIES WITH BASIL SYRUP *63*
RABARBARO ARROSTO E FRAGOLE CON SCIROPPO DI BASILICO

POACHED NECTARINE, PEACH AND FIG SALAD WITH LEMON AND PISTACHIOS *64*
PESCHENOCI, PESCHE E FICHI COTTI CON LIMONE E PISTACCHI

ORANGE AND MELON SALAD WITH RASPBERRY SAUCE *67*
MACEDONIA DI ARANCIA E MELONE CON SALSA DI LAMPONI

NUTS, BEANS & LEGUMES

BEAN SOUP *72*
ZUPPA DI FAGIOLI

GREEN BEANS WITH SESAME SEEDS *74*
FAGIOLINI CON SEMI DI SESAMO

PESTO GENOVESE 75

BEANS WITH ITALIAN SAUSAGES *77*
FAGIOLI CON SALSICCE ITALIANE

BROAD BEAN HUMMUS *78*

CREMA DI FAVE

CREAMY PENNETTE WITH WALNUTS *81*

PENNETTE CREMOSE ALLE NOCI

GREEN AND WHITE BEAN SALAD *82*

INSALATA DI FAGIOLINI E FAGIOLI

GREEN OLIVE AND HAZELNUT PESTO *83*

PESTO ALLE OLIVE VERDI E NOCCIOLE

VEGETABLES & SALADS

ARTICHOKE, ROAST PARSNIP AND WALNUT SALAD *91*

INSALATA DI CARCIOFI, PASTINACHE ARROSTITE E NOCI

ASPARAGUS WITH PISTACHIO ORANGE DRESSING *92*

ASPARAGI CON SALSA DI PISTACCHIO E ARANCIO

**BUTTERNUT SQUASH, RED ONION AND SPINACH SALAD
WITH A SESAME DRESSING** *94*

INSALATA DI ZUCCA, CIPOLLE ROSSE E SPINACI CON UNA SALSA DI SESAMO

FENNEL PURÉE *95*

PUREA DI FINOCCHIO

**CHARGRILLED SUMMER VEGETABLES WITH CHILLI
BASIL DRESSING** *96*

VERDURE GRIGLIATE CON SALSA PICCANTE E BASILICO

FIELD MUSHROOMS STUFFED WITH BACON AND SPINACH *98*

FUNGHI RIPIENI DI PANCETTA E SPINACI

PUMPKIN *MOSTARDA* *100*

MOSTARDA DI ZUCCA

PARMESAN MASHED POTATOES *102*

PUREA AL PARMIGIANO

POOR PEOPLE'S POTATOES *103*

PATATE DEI POVERI

PURPLE SPROUTING BROCCOLI WITH WATERCRESS
MAYONNAISE *104*
BROCCOLETTI CON MAIONESE AL CRESCIONE

TOMATO FENNEL SOUP *106*
ZUPPA DI POMODORO E FINOCCHIO

WILD GARLIC AND ROCKET SOUP *107*
ZUPPA DI AGLIO SELVATICO E RUCOLA

WARM RADICCHIO, SPINACH AND BASIL SALAD *109*
INSALATA DI RADICCHIO CALDI, SPINACI E BASILICO

ZUCCHINI STUFFED WITH RAGÙ *110*
ZUCCHINE RIPIENE AL RAGÙ

OLIVES & OLIVE OIL

CITRUS-MARINATED OLIVES *116*
OLIVE MARINATE AGLI AGRUMI

CHILLI OLIVE OIL *119*
OLIO D'OLIVA AL PEPERONCINO

ROSEMARY AND GARLIC OLIVE OIL *119*
OLIO D'OLIVA AL ROSMARINO ED AGLIO

OLIVE OIL ICE CREAM *120*
GELATO ALL'OLIO D'OLIVA

CHEESE, YOGHURT & EGGS

BLACKBERRY AND RASPBERRY YOGHURT ICE CREAM *127*
GELATO ALLO YOGURT DI MORE E LAMPONI

WATERCRESS AND HAZELNUT CRUMBED GOATS CHEESE SALAD *128*
INSALATA DI CRESCIONE, NOCCIOLE E FORMAGGIO DI CAPRA

EGGS *SOFFRITTO* *131*
UOVA AL FORNO CON VERDURE

POACHED APPLES STUFFED WITH GORGONZOLA *132*
MELE IN CAMICIA RIPIENE DI GORGONZOLA

BROAD BEAN AND PECORINO SALAD *134*
INSALATA DI FAVE E PECORINO

SORREL FLAN *135*
CROSTATA DI ACETOSELLA

FISH & SHELLFISH

CHARGRILLED DUBLIN BAY PRAWNS *140*
GAMBERONI ALLA GRIGLIA

COD WITH *SALMORIGLIO* *142*
MERLUZZO CON SALMORIGLIO

SWORDFISH WITH CHILLI AND ORANGE *143*
PESCE SPADA CON PEPERONCINO E ARANCIA

SCALLOPS WITH PROSCIUTTO AND BALSAMIC GLAZE *144*
CAPESANTE CON PROSCIUTTO E CREMA BALSAMICA

SEAFOOD STEW *146*
ZUPPA DI FRUTTI DI MARE

WHOLE BAKED SEA BASS WITH A RED PEPPER AND FENNEL
SAUCE *147*
SPIGOLA AL FORNO CON SALSA DI PEPERONI E FINOCCHI

TUNA WITH WHITE BEANS AND ARTICHOKES *149*
TONNO CON FAGIOLI E CARCIOFI

POULTRY & MEAT

MIXED *ANTIPASTO* PLATTER *154*
ANTIPASTO MISTO

SUPREME OF CHICKEN WITH ROCKET AND PARMESAN STUFFING *155*
POLLO RIPIENO DI RUCOLA E PARMIGIANO

CHICKEN WITH PROSECCO AND SHALLOTS *156*
POLLO CON PROSECCO E SCALOGNO

PANCETTA-WRAPPED CHICKEN THIGHS WITH
MOZZARELLA STUFFING *159*
COSCE DI POLLO AVVOLTI IN PANCETTA CON RIPIENO DI MOZZARELLA

SPATCHCOCK CHICKEN WITH 40 CLOVES OF GARLIC *160*
POLLO ALLA DIAVOLA CON 40 SPICCHI DI AGLIO

DATE AND HAZELNUT STUFFED PORK TENDERLOIN *162*
FILETTO DI MAIALE RIPIENO DI DATTERI E NOCCIOLE

ITALIAN WEDDING SOUP *163*
ZUPPA NUZIALE

SPARE RIBS WITH POLENTA CHIPS *164*
COSTINE CON PATATINE DI POLENTA

HERB-WRAPPED FILLET OF BEEF WITH
WILD MUSHROOM SAUCE *167*
FILETTO DI MANZO AVVOLTO NELLE ERBE CON SALSA DI FUNGHI SELVATICI

LAMB STEW WITH LEMON AND OLIVES *168*
SPEZZATINO DI AGNELLO CON LIMONE E OLIVE

PISTACHIO AND FIG CRUSTED RACK OF LAMB WITH TAPENADE *169*
CARRÈ DI AGNELLO IN CROSTA DI PISTACCHI E FICHI CON TAPENADE

SWEETS

ALMOND CAKE *174*
TORTA DI MANDORLE

CHOCOLATE BREADCRUMB AND ALMOND CAKE *176*
TORTA DI CIOCCOLATO, PANGRATTATO E MANDORLE

CHOCOLATE RICOTTA TART *178*
TORTA DI RICOTTA AL CIOCCOLATO

FRESH FRUIT TART *179*
CROSTATA DI FRUTTA FRESCA

DRINKS

CATHERINE FULVIO IS
THE PROPRIETOR OF THE
BALLYKNOCKEN HOUSE, FARM &
COOKERY SCHOOL IN WICKLOW. SHE
IS A PROLIFIC COOKERY WRITER,
A CHAMPION OF LOCAL FOODS AND
ONE OF IRELAND'S TOP TELEVISION
CULINARY STARS.
WWW.BALLYKNOCKEN.COM

DEDICATION

*To Charlotte and Rowan
for loving to laugh so much.
Vi amo
Mamma xx*

ACKNOWLEDGEMENTS

Thank you to Claudio, Charlotte and Rowan and all my friends and family for your wonderful support. You are the madness that keeps me sane!

To all of my colleagues here at Ballyknocken House & Cookery School, especially Rowena, Aoife, Mary and Gema. In particular a very special thanks to Sharon, who did a truly magnificent job styling the food for the photographs, and to Ella, who cooked it all so beautifully. That said, I blame you both for the extra 3kg I gained during those two months!

To Harry, our hugely talented photographer and not too bad of an Italian driver – just stay off the tram lines and out of the way of the old ladies next time!

To all at Gill & Macmillan, especially Fergal, Nicki, Catherine, Teresa, Ciara, Kristin, Paul, Peter and our designer, Graham. It's always a true pleasure to work with such a talented crew.

To my friends in Piedmont – Louise and Luca Garrone of Castello San Sebastiano and Maurizio Vellano from the wine resort Ca' San Sebastiano.

To Armando Borgatta, my mentor in the art of perfect Italian!

To Georgina and Majella, my beauty queens!

A special thanks to all our Italian friends and family, in particular the families Fulvio, Cucuru and Testagrossa in Palermo, Balestrate and Braciano.

Grazie Mille
Catherine

PROPS

Props supplied by

Ballyknocken Cookery School, Glenealy, Wicklow. Tel: 040 444 627
www.ballyknocken.com

Byrnes Giftware and Furniture (for Newbridge Jewellery), Main Street, Wicklow Town. Tel: 040 467 824

Arnotts, Henry Street, Dublin.
Tel: 01 805 0400 www.arnotts.ie

Strawbridge, Mt Usher Gardens, Ashford. Tel: 040 440 502 www.strawbridge.ie

Article, Powerscourt Townhouse, Dublin. Tel: 01 679 9268 www.articledublin.com

Find, Cow Lane, Temple Bar West, Dublin 2. Tel: 01 679 9790 www.findonline.ie

Meadows and Byrne, Dublin, Cork, Galway, Clare, Tipperary. Tel: 01 280 4554
www.meadowsandbyrne.ie

INTRODUCTION

Italian culture has had an enormous influence on the world, from artists such as Michelangelo and Caravaggio to creators such as Da Vinci and Marconi, from style icons such as Armani and Dolce & Gabbana to movie stars such as Sophia Loren and Rudolph Valentino, from Vespa to Ferrari and from Vivaldi to Verdi. But the greatest Italian culture is the food culture. It is the anchor that binds the people and their communities.

Food defines the Italian people. It comes as no surprise that the Slow Food movement was started in Italy, where 'fast food' does not exist – all food is to be savoured and enjoyed, especially in the company of friends and family.

There are many things that intrigue me about Italian food culture. How do they have time for all this food? Why do they have such strict rules and routine around food? With long, leisurely lunches, dishes of pasta richly coated in sauces, pizzas laden with mozzarella and glugs of olive oil, how is it that Italy is one of the slimmest nations in Europe? And most importantly, how can we enjoy these delicious recipes and savour some of *la dolce vita* here at home? That is what this book is about.

Let me tell you a story about Italian lifestyle and food. It's a beautiful summer evening and I'm out shopping in our local town of Balestrate in Sicily. A new furniture shop has just opened up in the town square and I have a long look in the window. As I expected, the shop is beautifully laid out with all the elegance of Italian interior style. My eye catches a fabulous mahogany dining table and matching chairs, fully dressed with the best glassware and china.

Imagine my surprise when just after 8 p.m., when the shops close, I pass again and I stop in shock, as the table I had just admired was now fully complete with diners. The staff had locked the doors and sat down to enjoy this magnificent table by having a meal together in the shop window, totally oblivious to life beyond their own company and their enjoyment of their meal.

Then it dawned on me. This is Italy, where people live to eat, not eat to live. The more I considered this fact, the more clarity I got. I'd seen for myself that work stops when friends arrive – unplanned departures are made from offices in favour of the local coffee shop and work continues thereafter, until another friend or family member arrives. In other words, work fits around life and not life around work. And that's logical, since offices open at around 8 a.m. and close at 8 p.m., so work has to fit around life. It's frowned upon to talk business over lunch. Eating is about the company, the food, the laughter, chatter and sheer pleasure and should not be soured by discussions of work.

In order to eat like an Italian, we need to recondition ourselves to live like Italians. It might seem a little stressful to fit into our lifestyle of long commutes to and from work, college and kids. We all have such full days, but then, so do the Italians. As a family here in Wicklow, we make a point of sitting down and breaking bread together. It would be idyllic to do this every day, but realistically, we insist on four days together every week and include our extended family and friends in this too.

One thing I've learned is that work has to fit around life. I struggled for years trying to separate work from my life, but I constantly felt guilty about not spending enough time with my family. I realised that this was leading me nowhere and now I relax into work and prioritise life and it feels very empowering.

ITALIAN FOOD CULTURE: SHOPPING AND INGREDIENTS

Locally sourced food is the backbone of Italian food. Recipes are regional too and it's unusual for people to cook non-regional dishes, especially for family gatherings, otherwise there might be a grandmother or two who would pass comment!

In Balestrate, our local town, it's not uncommon for the women to shop for ingredients twice per day – for lunch and for dinner. Now that really is the epitome of freshness! It's also common for the farmers to drive through the towns in their three-wheeled scooter trucks laden with produce from their farms, shouting their arrival through the loudspeaker positioned atop the van. The ladies purchase from their balconies by lowering a basket on a rope to collect the fresh melons, tomatoes, oranges and lemons. Shopping is also a social occasion to meet other locals and a chance to get daily exercise. I understand that this probably isn't an option for most of us, but buying local, fresh produce where possible and even growing your own in little pots or plots is something to aim for.

As you travel through Italy, you learn very quickly that everyone has a passion for food and also has a strong opinion about where the best recipe or ingredient can be sourced. A few years back, our car broke down near Pachino, which is the famous tomato-producing area of Italy. The Pachino tomatoes are cherry-like, sweet and irresistible. We had to get the car towed back to Catania airport and arrange a replacement, and it was a long three hours once the driver realised my interest in food! He spent the journey telling me that Pachino tomatoes weren't the best in Italy, but that actually the ones from his village were. Next to come was his opinion on olive oil, oranges, grapes, lemons ... I couldn't get a word in edgeways, which is unusual for me! But it is this passion and inquisitiveness about food that drives the Italians to create the best dishes. There is a lesson here.

MEALTIMES AND MEALS

Breakfast usually consists of a cappuccino and a brioche or bread with butter and/or some local jam. In Sicily in the summer, brioche and *granita* (a flavoured iced drink, which might be coffee flavoured) is most common, as it is considered too hot to sip a cappuccino.

Lunch is the main meal of the day and is usually somewhere between 12 and 1 p.m. In fact, the restaurants stop serving at around 2.30 p.m., as people stick rigidly to mealtimes and demand outside of this is unheard of, unless by tourists.

A two-course lunch is most common midweek, but Sunday lunch is a major meal and involves the extended family. It's customary for family members to bring a gift of a cooked dish and the preparations for Sunday lunch commence the day before.

A typical meal would start with *l'antipasto* – perhaps olives, local cured meats, cheeses and bread.

This is followed by *il primo*, which is the pasta or rice course. Pasta servings are smaller than we might think, as there are still many more courses to follow.

Il secondo is the meat or fish course. As meat or fish might not be eaten every day, this is a special course. After this comes *il contoro* – the side dish. *Contori* are always vegetables in season and often salads. *Secondi* are usually eaten first, then *contori*. A side dish that I really enjoyed at Sunday lunch in the Fulvio household in Palermo was a simple raw fennel bulb, which was passed around the table and we each pulled a layer off and chewed it. It was so refreshing after the fish course. Then fresh fruit platters arrive – again, always whatever is in season, followed by dried nuts and fruits in the winter (dried figs and dates are especially delicious).

After that, coffee is made and *il dolce* – a cake from the local bakery – is produced. A pistachio and lemon sponge cake with a sweet ricotta filling was one of the most delicious I've ever had. And finally, out come the chocolates and the *ammazzacaffè*, which means 'coffee-killer', a liqueur, which could be anything from homemade nocino (walnut liqueur) to limoncello.

All of this is often followed by a promenade in one's Sunday best clothes – a lovely gentle stroll through the town or countryside, meeting other locals along the way. After all, seven courses requires a stretching of the body, and it feels so much better after a large meal than collapsing on the sofa in front of the television! Exercise is simply integrated into the Italians' day, whether it's walking to school or the shops, promenading after a large lunch or dancing in the evening.

Dinner is at 8 p.m. and is really more like supper. It's a much lighter meal, usually only one course, and might be made up of the leftovers from lunch.

Drinks with meals consist of wine and water, or maybe a beer with pizza. Children are allowed a soft drink (generally not milk, as that is deemed to affect the flavours of the food and digestion). We enjoy a similar routine to this for our family mealtimes, especially the large family gatherings on a Sunday. It's a time to catch up and chat, and when I think about it, it's not unlike the lifestyle of my parents and grandparents years ago – except I recall that my granddad always drank tea brimming with milk and sugar with his main course. I wonder what the Italians would think of that?

THE MEDITERRANEAN AND ITALIAN DIET

Recognised by UNESCO, the Mediterranean diet is arguably the healthiest diet in the world.

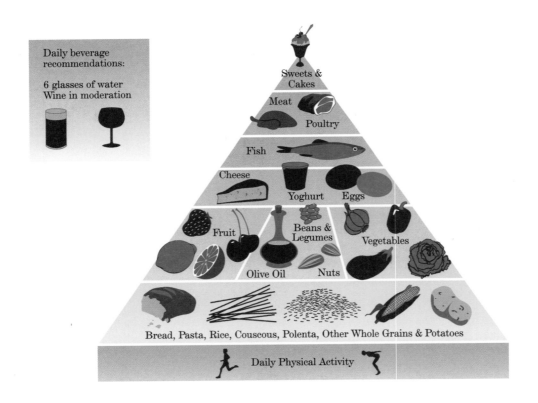

The inclusion of daily recommended amounts of olive oil, beans, nuts and legumes in the Mediterranean diet is in clear contrast to our diet, where we don't include many of these. In Italy, red meat is eaten in smaller quantities, while fish is the more popular protein. Not surprisingly, the quantity of carbohydrates consumed in Italy on a daily basis exceeds ours. Wine, noted 'in moderation', is a recognised part of the diet.

The Mediterranean and Italian diet is characterised by a nutritional model, as on p. xviii, that comprises fresh seasonal ingredients, an abundance of cereals, fresh fruits and vegetables, generous amounts of olive oil, pulses and nuts and moderate amounts of fish and meats. UNESCO also recognised that this diet encompasses more than just food – it promotes social interaction, thereby giving full credit to the lifestyle. In my opinion, the Italian diet and approach to food is the solution to long-lasting health and happiness, so I have structured this book by each section of the food pyramid. Just try to eat a few more from the Vegetables and Salads chapter and a few less from the Sweets chapter!

It's pretty realistic for everyone to embrace this lifestyle and food culture by enjoying our very own local, seasonally fresh produce, prioritising our mealtimes by making them routine and including our friends and family, taking daily exercise and a drink in moderation.

I hope you enjoy these recipes from Italy, then relax and savour the wonderful flavours of freshly prepared food while enjoying the company of others. It is the recipe for a good life.

BREAD, PASTA,
RICE & COUSCOUS

CARBOHYDRATES

While we're all warned to cut the carbs, the Italians relish in them – and in their slimness! It just doesn't seem fair. What's evident to me is the Italian approach to 'everything in moderation'. Their carb portions are definitely smaller than ours and 'stop when you are full' is also an Italian mantra … but sometimes it just tastes so good!

For Italians, carbs incorporate bread, pasta, rice, polenta and couscous. As with all things Italian, there are strong regional differences. For example, couscous is a staple in Sicily, whereas polenta is in the north. Even the type of flour used in the bread differs, from the durum wheat in the south to the *grano tenero* or even chestnut flour in the north.

BREAD

Bread-making is a serious business, with many types having been awarded DOP status (*Denominazione di origine protetta*, or protected designation of origin) by the EU. DOP status protects the names of regional foods and strictly outlines how they must be made. One of my favourite DOP breads is the *Pane di Altamura* from the province of Bari in Puglia. Golden in colour, it has a wonderful chewy crust (which must be 3mm thick, by the way).

Breads vary from region to region and there are over 350 recognised types of bread. The local *panificio* will produce regional breads, pizza sold in slices and focaccia and may also make sandwiches (*panini*). Bread is usually sold by weight.

Solina, our friend and local baker in Sicily, runs Panificio Testagrossa, where she produces the most delicious *sfincione* once a week. The queues build up down the street in anticipation of the delicious, thick, pizza-like bread coming out of the oven and it sells out within minutes. She also makes lots of biscotti, many using almonds or coconut as a base, and in the late autumn she makes the amazing traditional marzipan fruit, which is an enormous amount of work but very popular as Christmas gifts.

I particularly like the *Pane Siciliano*, which is made with yellow durum wheat flour. A family favourite is Roman pizza, especially *pizza bianca*, which can be turned into a delicious sandwich with prosciutto and cheese (see page 9).

'*Fare la scarpetta*' is usually heard when any pasta sauce remains on the plate. There is no direct English translation, but it broadly means 'to do the little shoe' – it really means to clean your plate with the bread. We use a piece of the bread shaped like a mini shoehorn to mop up the sauce from the plate.

Leabharlanna Poibli Chathair Bhaile Átha Cliath
Dublin City Public Libraries

PASTA

A couple of years ago, I had the pleasure of meeting the author Oretta Zanini De Vita at her home in Rome. She had just received the James Beard Foundation Award for her book *The Encyclopaedia of Pasta*. Imagine my surprise when she told me that there are over one thousand types of pasta in Italy, and as expected, many of them are regional.

She told me the story of an American tourist who purchased a *pasta lungo*, which is a long spaghetti pasta, 1 metre in length, from an artisan producer in Puglia. The lady managed to get the pasta home to the US totally intact. When she went to cook it she had a moment of panic, as she had no saucepan large enough to cook it in. So she telephoned the pasta maker in Puglia, who split his sides laughing, only to tell her that she needed to break the pasta to fit in the saucepan. But this is probably the only time when pasta gets broken or cut!

Aside from all the mainstream pastas, there are the artisan versions, including *alla chittara*, so named because the pasta is like the strings of a guitar.

Some regional dishes are always made with the same pasta shapes. *Penne all'Arrabbiata*, *Fettuccine all'Alfredo* and *Bucatini all'Amatriciana* are all classic Roman recipes and are prepared with the pasta names in their titles. Heavy sauces with pieces of meat are usually served with wide noodles such as pappardelle or tagliatelle or with short tubular shapes such as penne or fusilli.

In the south of Italy, sauces tend to be made with olive oil and are usually served with dried plain wheat pasta such as spaghetti and vermicelli. These long, thin shapes are traditionally served with tomato and seafood sauces, most of which are made with olive oil and with a light vegetable sauce. Grated cheese isn't normally used in these sauces, nor for sprinkling on top. In the north, butter and cream are used in the sauces and they go well with egg pasta, which absorbs the butter and cream and makes the sauce cling to it.

PASTA SHAPE	PASTA NAME	IDEAL SAUCES
Long and thin	Angel hair, vermicelli	Oil-based, light, thin broth
Long and wide	Fettuccine, spaghetti, linguine, pappardelle	Light cream sauces, Alfredo sauce, some meat sauces and light tomato sauces
Short and chunky pasta	Rigatoni, shells, elbow, fusilli, penne, farfalle, anelli (Sicilian rounds)	Chunky sauce, meat sauces, shaped pasta casseroles, salads
Tiny	Ditalini, small shells, alphabets	Soups, stews and salads

COMBINING THE PASTA AND SAUCE

To cook pasta, bring a large saucepan of water to the boil and add salt. Add the pasta and stir. Olive oil only needs to be added to the water for egg pastas, since it is stickier pasta.

A clever rule that I learned from Claudio's aunt is 2, 4, 400: for every 400g of pasta, use 4 litres of boiling water and 2 tsp of salt. It is very important that the pasta is cooked *al dente*, as it will absorb the sauce. If overcooked, the sauce slides off the pasta, making it a tasteless dish.

When draining the pasta, quickly sit the colander back on top of the saucepan to catch the remaining cooking liquid. This is used later to loosen sticky pasta or to thin out a rich sauce. The pasta is then added to the sauce.

FLOUR

In Italy, flour is classified into categories depending on how finely milled the flour is and how much of the bran and texture have been removed.

Tipo doppio zero, '00', is highly refined and soft and is normally used for making egg pasta, pizza, biscotti and breads, whereas durum means 'hard' in Latin and the species is one of the hardest of all wheats. It has a high protein content and is especially good for making a plain pasta.

The fame of Sicilian durum wheat goes back to when the Greeks inhabited Sicily and the island was given the title of the 'grain basket of the Mediterranean'. In most areas of Sicily, durum wheat is used in bread-making. Other flours include chickpea and chestnut, which are used regionally.

FOCACCIA WITH CARAMELISED RED ONIONS

FOCACCIA CON CIPOLLE ROSSE CARAMELLATE / MAKES 2 MEDIUM LOAVES OR 1 LARGE

THEY SAY YOU CAN SELL YOUR HOUSE SIMPLY ON THE AROMA OF BREAD BAKING. PERSONALLY, I WOULDN'T LET ANYONE THROUGH THE DOOR OF MY HOUSE WHILE THIS BREAD IS IN THE OVEN. IT'S TOO GOOD TO SHARE!

1½ tsp dried yeast
caster sugar
225ml lukewarm water
   (approximately)

350g strong white flour
extra virgin olive oil
1 tsp salt
2 medium red onions, finely chopped

rosemary (or sage), finely chopped,
   to taste
coarse sea salt

1 Mix the yeast and 2 tsp of sugar in the lukewarm water and allow it to activate – when the yeast froths, it's ready to use.
2 Sieve the flour into a mixing bowl. Add 3 tbsp olive oil, salt and the yeast mixture.
3 Mix to a loose dough, adding more flour or water as required, until just combined. Knead for about 5 minutes. Leave the dough to rise in a well-oiled bowl covered with plastic wrap until the dough has trebled in size and is springy to the touch, which will take about 2 hours. It will rise best in a warm location, such as a hot press or near a cooker or oven.
4 Meanwhile, to caramelise the red onions, heat a saucepan with olive oil, add the onions and 2 tbsp sugar and allow to sauté slowly for 8–9 minutes, until the onions have softened. Set aside.
5 When the bread has risen, knock it back and tip it out onto an oiled surface. Knead it again by hand for 2–3 minutes.
6 Divide the dough into 2 pieces and roll out into rectangles 1cm thick (or just make 1 large rectangle). Put the rectangles onto an oiled baking sheet and make indentations with your fingertips. Brush the surface generously with olive oil. Sprinkle the onions, finely chopped rosemary (or sage) and coarse sea salt on top. Allow to rise again for 1–1 ½ hours, until doubled in size.
7 Preheat the oven to 230°C/fan 210°C/gas 8. Bake for 5 minutes, then reduce the temperature to 200°C/fan 180°C/gas 6 and bake for a further 10 minutes. Allow to cool before serving.

 KEEPING IT LOCAL: MAKE AN IRISH FOCACCIA USING A SODA BREAD RECIPE WITH GLAZED ONIONS AND THYME AS A TOPPING.

CIABATTA

THE UNIQUE FLAVOUR OF CIABATTA IS ITS SLIGHT SOURNESS, WHICH IS ACHIEVED BY MAKING A BIGA, OR SPONGE, IN ADVANCE. DON'T BE PUT OFF BY LENGTHY BREAD RECIPES, THEY ARE SO WORTHWHILE. TRY ADDING 8 SLICED BLACK OLIVES TO THE MIX BEFORE THE SECOND RISING FOR A SCRUMPTIOUS TWIST.

FOR THE SPONGE:
100ml warm water
1/2 tsp dried yeast
125g '00' flour

FOR THE BREAD:
1 1/2 tsp dried yeast
2 tbsp warm milk
200ml warm water

1 tbsp olive oil
350g '00' flour, plus extra for
   kneading
1 tsp salt

1 To make the sponge, combine the warm water and the yeast in a large bowl and allow it to stand for 5 minutes, then stir in the flour. Cover with plastic wrap and let it stand in a cool, draught-free place for 12 hours.

2 To make the bread, combine the yeast and milk in a small bowl and allow to stand for 5 minutes.

3 Attach the dough hook to an electric mixer and slowly blend together the sponge, milk and yeast, water, olive oil and flour at a low speed until the flour is mixed to a sticky dough. Increase the speed to medium, add the salt and knead the dough for 4 minutes.

4 Scrape out the dough into an oiled bowl, cover with plastic wrap and leave to rise in a warm room until it doubles in size, which will take about 2 hours.

5 Line 2 baking trays with parchment paper or dust with semolina.

6 When the dough has doubled in size, place it onto a well-floured surface and gently knead for 1 minute. Cut the dough in half, transfer to the lined baking trays and shape into long rectangular loaves. Dust the tops with flour or semolina and cover with a damp kitchen towel. Leave to rise in a warm room until almost doubled in size, which should take about 1 $^1/_2$ hours.

7 Preheat the oven to 210°C/fan 190°C/gas 6. Place the loaves in the oven and bake for 15–18 minutes, until they're a pale golden colour. Transfer the loaves onto a cooling rack.

KEEPING IT LOCAL: THE '00' FLOUR IS IDEAL FOR THIS BREAD, BUT IF THAT'S UNAVAILABLE, THIS RECIPE ALSO WORKS NICELY WITH ODLUM'S STRONG FLOUR.

ROMAN-STYLE PIZZA BIANCA

PIZZA BIANCA / MAKES ONE 30CM X 40CM RECTANGLE

WHEN IN ROME, DO AS THE ROMANS DO, SO EAT PIZZA – OR RATHER, MAKE PIZZA. THE BIANCA IS A GOOD CHOICE
TO USE WHEN PREPARING SANDWICHES OR TO SERVE WITH A DELICIOUS BOWL OF SOUP.

1 rounded tsp dried yeast	extra virgin olive oil
1/2 tsp caster sugar	1/2 tsp sea salt
150ml lukewarm water (more if required)	2 garlic cloves, sliced
250g Italian '00' or strong white flour	1 tbsp chopped rosemary

1 Mix the yeast and sugar in the lukewarm water and allow the yeast to activate. When the yeast is frothy, it's ready to use.
2 Sieve the flour into a mixing bowl and add 1 tsp olive oil, the salt and the yeast mixture. Mix to a loose dough, adding more flour or water as required. Knead until the dough is very pliable, which should take about 5 minutes using the dough hook of a stand mixer or 5–8 minutes by hand.
3 Leave the dough to rise in a well-oiled bowl covered with plastic wrap until the dough has doubled in size and is springy to the touch, which will take about 2 hours. This will rise best in a warm, draught-free place.
4 Preheat the oven to 230°C/fan 210°C/gas 8. Lightly oil a baking sheet.
5 When the dough has risen, knock it back and place onto a lightly floured surface. Knead it again by hand for 2–3 minutes. Roll out or stretch the dough as thinly as possible onto the oiled pizza pan. Brush the pizza lightly with olive oil. Toss the garlic and rosemary in a generous amount of olive oil so that the garlic doesn't burn while it's cooking and spread the mixture over the pizza, leaving a 1cm rim around the edge.
6 Bake for 5–6 minutes and drizzle over more olive oil when it comes straight from the oven.

KEEPING IT LOCAL: TOP WITH YOUR FAVOURITE ARTISAN INGREDIENT SPREAD OVER A TOMATO SAUCE,
SUCH AS STONE AGE FARM'S AIR-DRIED HAM AND SLICES OF THE FRUITY DURRUS CHEESE.

FRESH FIG AND PROSCIUTTO PANINO

PANINO CON FICHI FRESCHI E PROSCIUTTO / MAKES 4

PANINO IS ALSO REFERRED TO AS *TRAMEZZINO*. THE NAME WAS INTRODUCED BY THE FASCISTS, WHO DISLIKED THE USE OF THE WORD 'SANDWICH', WHICH HAD BEEN CREEPING INTO THE ITALIAN LANGUAGE. *TRA* MEANS 'IN BETWEEN' AND *MEZZO* MEANS 'MIDDLE', I.E. SOMETHING IN THE MIDDLE OF THE BREAD.

½ *pizza bianca* (see page 9)
extra virgin olive oil
salt and freshly ground black pepper
8 tsp basil pesto
rocket leaves, washed
4 prosciutto slices
4 fresh figs, sliced
8 cherry tomatoes, halved
100g buffalo mozzarella, sliced

1 Place the bread on a board and cut into 4 rectangles, then slice in half across the middle. Drizzle half of the bread slices generously with the olive oil. Sprinkle with salt and freshly ground black pepper and spread some of the pesto on top.
2 Place the rocket on the bread and add the prosciutto slices. Arrange the figs on top, followed by the tomato halves and mozzarella slices.
3 Drizzle a little more pesto over and end with another splash of the oil. Top with the remaining slices of *pizza bianca*.

 KEEPING IT LOCAL: SLICES OF O'NEILL'S DRY CURED HAM WITH ROASTED PEPPERS ARE A WINNER FOR SANDWICHES.

BUCATINI WITH AMATRICIANA SAUCE

BUCATINI ALL'AMATRICIANA / SERVES 4

BUCATINI IS THE PERFECT ACCOMPANIMENT FOR SOAKING UP THIS DELICIOUS SAUCE. A ROMAN STAPLE, THIS SAUCE TRADITIONALLY USES THE FATTIER *GUANCIALE*, THE PIG CHEEK, AS ITS BASE INSTEAD OF PANCETTA AND THE CHILLI IS OPTIONAL.

2 tbsp extra virgin olive oil
250g pancetta, diced
1 medium red chilli, diced
2 garlic cloves, sliced
400g tinned chopped tomatoes
100ml white wine
1 tsp caster sugar
salt and freshly ground black pepper
350g bucatini
120g Pecorino Romano, grated
basil and parsley leaves, to garnish

1 To make the sauce, heat a large saucepan with the olive oil. Sauté the pancetta over a low heat for 7 minutes. Remove from the pan and set aside.
2 Add the chilli and sauté for 2–3 minutes. Add the garlic and cook for 1 minute.
3 Stir in the tomatoes, white wine and sugar. Return the pancetta to the sauce, then season with salt and freshly ground black pepper. Simmer uncovered for about 35 minutes.
4 Meanwhile, cook the bucatini according to the instructions on the package.
5 Toss the drained, cooked pasta into the sauce. Sprinkle over the Pecorino, garnish with basil and parsley leaves and serve.

KEEPING IT LOCAL: COMBINE UMMERA DRY CURED BACON RASHERS WITH THE EARTHY TANG OF MOUNT CALLAN FARMHOUSE CHEESE FOR A WONDERFUL IRISH VERSION OF THIS DISH.

FETTUCCINE WITH PORCINI AND HAZELNUTS

FETTUCCINE CON PORCINI E NOCCIOLE / SERVES 4

THE PORCINI HAVE SUCH DEPTH OF FLAVOUR AND THEY ARE ALWAYS AVAILABLE, DRIED, IN EVERY GREENGROCER IN ITALY. AS AN ALTERNATIVE, YOUR GREENGROCER WILL HAVE TRAYS OF LOCAL WILD MUSHROOMS THAT CAN BE COOKED FROM FRESH.

350g fettuccine

2 tbsp extra virgin olive oil

2 shallots, finely chopped

2 garlic cloves, crushed

1/2 tsp thyme, chopped

100g dried porcini, rehydrated in 75ml warm water, then chopped

150ml cream

75ml white wine

salt and freshly ground black pepper

3 tbsp roughly chopped hazelnuts

1 Cook the pasta according to the instructions on the package.

2 Meanwhile, heat the oil in a saucepan over a low heat. Add the shallots and sauté for about 5 minutes. Add the garlic and thyme and cook for a further 3 minutes. Add the porcini and the liquid, followed by the cream and white wine, and stir. Season to taste and simmer for 2 minutes.

3 Add the drained, cooked pasta to the sauce. Sprinkle over the hazelnuts and serve immediately.

KEEPING IT LOCAL: WE GET SOME WONDERFUL RIB EYE STEAK FROM OUR LOCAL BUTCHER FOOD HERO, ROBERT CULLEN, AND SERVE IT WITH THE PORCINI SAUCE FOR A SCRUMPTIOUS DINNER.

LINGUINE PRIMAVERA

SERVES 4

I LOVE SPRING, AS I GET TO USE THIS WONDERFUL RECIPE WITH THE FRESH, BRIGHT, YOUNG VEGETABLES. IT JUST FEELS HEALTHY AND FILLED WITH VITAMINS.

350g linguine or your favourite pasta

2 tbsp extra virgin olive oil

2 leeks, finely sliced

2 garlic cloves, sliced

100ml white wine

12 asparagus spears, sliced

100g peas

1 lemon, zest only

150g crème fraîche

75g baby spinach leaves, washed and trimmed

3 tbsp chopped basil

1 tbsp chopped tarragon

salt and freshly ground black pepper

freshly grated Parmesan, to serve

4 mint leaves, to garnish

1 Cook the pasta according to the instructions on the package. Retain some of the cooking liquid for later.

2 Heat the olive oil in a large saucepan over a medium heat. Add the leeks and sauté for about 4 minutes. Add the garlic and sauté for 1 minute. Stir in the white wine and simmer for about 1 minute, then add the asparagus, peas and lemon zest. Cover and simmer until just tender. Add the crème fraîche, spinach, basil and tarragon.

3 Add the cooked, drained pasta to the sauce and thin with some of the retained pasta liquid as required. Season to taste. Sprinkle with grated Parmesan and garnish with mint leaves.

KEEPING IT LOCAL: TAKE A TRIP TO THE QUAYS FOR SOME LOCALLY CAUGHT PRAWNS – WE SOURCE JUICY PRAWNS FROM HOWTH AND KILMORE QUAY. SAUTÉ THE PRAWNS WITH BUTTER AND A SPRITZ OF LEMON JUICE TO ENHANCE THIS DELIGHTFUL PASTA DISH.

SPAGHETTI WITH FRUITS OF THE SEA

SPAGHETTI AI FRUTTI DI MARE / SERVES 4

THIS SAUCE HAS RED CHILLIES ADDED, SO IF YOU AREN'T A GREAT FAN OF THE HEAT, IT'S NO PROBLEM TO OMIT THEM. AND HOW ABOUT ADDING A ROSÉ WINE INSTEAD OF THE WHITE FOR A LITTLE BLUSH?

350g spaghetti

extra virgin olive oil

1 1/2 red chillies, diced

2 garlic cloves, finely sliced

1 lemon, zest only

100ml white wine

500g clams

500g mussels

200g prawns, tails on

2 squid pouches, sliced into rings

2 tbsp chopped parsley

lemon wedges, to serve

salt and freshly ground black pepper

1 Cook the spaghetti according to the instructions on the package.
2 Heat a little olive oil in a large saucepan over a low heat. Add the red chillies and sauté for 2 minutes, then add the garlic and lemon zest and cook for 1 minute more. Pour in the wine and seasoning and simmer for 2 minutes.
3 Stir in the clams, mussels, prawns and squid rings. Place a lid on the saucepan and cook for about 3 minutes, until the clams and mussels have opened. Keep shaking the pot. Discard any clams or mussels that remain closed.
4 Stir in some of the parsley and add the cooked, drained spaghetti to the seafood. Serve in wide bowls with the lemon wedges and sprinkle over the remaining parsley.

KEEPING IT LOCAL: FISH OUT OF WATER, A LOCAL COMPANY HERE IN WICKLOW, PREPARES SOME EXQUISITE SMOKED OYSTERS AND MUSSELS, WHICH ARE ALSO DELICIOUS IN THIS RECIPE.

FARFALLE WITH RED PEPPER SAUCE

FARFALLE CON SALSA DI PEPERONI ROSSI / SERVES 4

I HAD THIS VERSATILE SAUCE OVER PASTA FOR LUNCH IN A SMALL RESTAURANT IN MILAN MANY YEARS AGO AND JUST HAD TO RECREATE IT AT HOME. IT'S ONE OF THOSE SAUCES THAT SEEM TO COMPLEMENT MOST FOODS. IT'S GREAT OVER STEAMED FISH AND EQUALLY TASTY OVER ROASTED GARLIC AND COURGETTES.

350g farfalle
1 tbsp extra virgin olive oil
3 shallots, finely chopped
1 tbsp tomato purée
100ml white wine
2 red peppers, roasted and chopped
50g crème fraîche
200ml fresh cream
salt and freshly ground black pepper
100g ricotta salata (or feta), crumbled, to serve
chives, to garnish

1 Cook the pasta according to the instructions on the package.
2 In the meantime, prepare the sauce. Heat the oil in a medium saucepan over a low heat and sauté the shallots until softened. Add the tomato purée and cook for 1 minute. Add the white wine and cook for a further 2–3 minutes. Add the roasted peppers and cook for 1–2 minutes, then stir in the crème fraîche and cream.
3 Remove from the heat and allow to cool slightly. Remove half the sauce and blend it to a purée, then mix both back together again. Season to taste.
4 Toss the drained, cooked pasta into the sauce, sprinkle over the crumbled ricotta salata and garnish with some chive lengths on top.

KEEPING IT LOCAL: THIS SAUCE IS ESPECIALLY TASTY SPOONED OVER STUFFED LOCAL FREE-RANGE CHICKEN BREASTS WRAPPED WITH LOCAL DRY CURED BACON.

ORECCHIETTE WITH FENNEL SAUSAGES AND BROCCOLI

ORECCHIETTE CON SALSA BARESE / SERVES 4

STRAIGHT FROM THE HEEL OF ITALY, THIS RECIPE HAS ITS ROOTS IN BARI, PUGLIA, BUT I FIRST HAD IT AT A GLAMOROUS SUNDAY LUNCH IN CLAUDIO'S AUNTIE LINA'S HOME IN PALERMO. I NEVER KNEW THAT BROCCOLI AND PASTA COMBINED COULD TASTE SO GOOD.

3 tbsp extra virgin olive oil

300g Italian fennel sausage

1 leek, finely sliced

3 garlic cloves, finely chopped

2 anchovies, chopped

350g tender stem broccoli

150ml white wine

salt and freshly ground black pepper

350g orecchiette

4 tbsp freshly grated Pecorino

1 To prepare the sauce, heat some of the olive oil in a frying pan over a medium heat and fry the sausages until cooked through. Remove from the pan, slice thinly on the diagonal and set aside.
2 Heat the rest of the olive oil in the saucepan, then add the leek and sauté for 5 minutes, until softened but not brown. Add the garlic and anchovies and cook for 1 minute. Add the broccoli and white wine and sauté for 10 minutes, until the broccoli has softened. Season to taste. Add the sausages back to the pan and heat through.
3 Meanwhile, cook the orecchiette according to the instructions on the package.
4 Drain the orecchiette, reserving some of the cooking liquid. Add the orecchiette to the sauce. Add 3–4 tbsp of the cooking liquid to the sauce if you feel it's too thick. Season to taste, then sprinkle over the Pecorino and serve immediately.

KEEPING IT LOCAL: TRY CROWE'S FARM ITALIAN SAUSAGES FROM TIPPERARY IN THIS RECIPE. THEY ARE DELICIOUS

SPAGHETTI WITH GARLIC AND OLIVE OIL

SPAGHETTI ALL' AGLIO E OLIO / SERVES 4

THIS IS A CLASSIC DISH THAT MOST ITALIAN MEN KNOW HOW TO COOK. IT'S ALSO KNOWN AS LOVER'S PASTA, AS IT'S QUICK AND EASY – READ INTO THAT AS YOU WISH!

350g spaghetti
75ml extra virgin olive oil
2 garlic cloves, finely sliced
1 dried chilli, chopped
salt and freshly ground black pepper
4 tbsp freshly grated Pecorino, to serve (optional)

1 Cook the spaghetti according to the instructions on the package. Reserve a little of the cooking liquid.
2 Meanwhile, heat the oil in a saucepan over a low heat. Add the garlic and the chilli and sauté for 1 minute, taking care not to let the garlic burn, then take the pan off the heat.
3 When the spaghetti is done, drain it and stir it into the sauce. Loosen with the reserved cooking liquid as required and season to taste. Sprinkle over the Pecorino, if using, and serve.

 KEEPING IT LOCAL: TRY MILL HOUSE SHEEP'S CHEESE FROM TULLAMORE INSTEAD OF THE PECORINO.

NEAPOLITAN CHRISTMAS EVE SPAGHETTI WITH WALNUTS

U SPAGHETT' ANATALINA / SERVES 4

DURING THE WEEKS BEFORE CHRISTMAS, WONDERFUL FRESH WALNUTS ARRIVE IN THE SHOPS. THIS WAS A RECIPE FOR 'POOR FOLKS' AND IT ILLUSTRATES HOW ITALIANS RESPECT THEIR INGREDIENTS. IT IS SIMPLE, PURE DELICIOUSNESS. DICED AUBERGINE CAN BE ADDED, BUT BEAR IN MIND THAT THE COOKING TIME WOULD BE LONGER.

350g spaghetti
100ml extra virgin olive oil
4 garlic cloves, very finely sliced
6 anchovies
150g walnuts, lightly toasted and chopped
salt and freshly ground black pepper
2 tbsp chopped flat-leaf parsley, to garnish

1 Cook the pasta according to the instructions on the package.
2 Heat the oil in a large saucepan over a low heat. Add the garlic and sauté for 1 minute, taking care not to burn the garlic. Add the anchovies and gently mash them with a fork so they dissolve in the oil.
3 Drain the pasta and reserve some of the cooking liquid. Add the cooked, drained pasta to the sauce. Stir in some of the cooking liquid to loosen the pasta and return to the heat.
4 Add the walnuts and cook for a further 1–2 minutes, then season to taste. Add the parsley and Merry Christmas!

KEEPING IT LOCAL: BRING MORE COLOUR TO THIS DISH BY ADDING FRESHLY STEAMED LOCALLY GROWN BROCCOLI FLORETS.

CHEESY MACARONI BAKE

PASTICCIO DI MACCHERONI / SERVES 4

BEING A ONE-POT DISH, THIS GREAT OVEN BAKE IS ALWAYS POPULAR. FOR A SLIGHTLY HEALTHIER VERSION, OMIT THE MOZZARELLA AND SPRINKLE OVER SOME TOASTED BREADCRUMBS MIXED WITH HERBS AND GRATED PARMESAN.

350g macaroni

50g butter

3 tbsp flour

200ml milk

5 tbsp freshly grated Parmesan

1 1/2 tsp chopped fresh oregano or 1 tsp dried oregano

100g mascarpone

pinch of nutmeg

salt and freshly ground black pepper

100g buffalo mozzarella, thinly sliced

4–5 basil leaves, torn

1 Preheat the oven to 180°C/fan 160°C/gas 4 and butter a medium gratin dish.

2 Cook the macaroni according to the instructions on the package. Drain, reserving some of the cooking liquid, and set aside.

3 To make the sauce, combine the butter and flour in a saucepan and cook, stirring over a low heat, for 4–5 minutes. Add the milk gradually, stirring most of the time, to form a thick sauce. Add the Parmesan and oregano.

4 Pour the cooked, drained pasta into a large bowl and add about 4 tbsp of the pasta cooking liquid. Stir in the Parmesan sauce and add in the mascarpone and nutmeg. Season to taste, then mix well and pour into the buttered gratin dish and top with the mozzarella.

5 Bake for 20–25 minutes, until golden and bubbling. Allow to stand for 5–10 minutes before serving. Garnish with the torn basil leaves and serve.

KEEPING IT LOCAL: ROAST ONE OF BERTRAM SALTER'S CARLOW FREE RANGE CHICKENS FOR SUNDAY LUNCH AND USE THE LEFTOVERS, SHREDDED AND MIXED IN WITH THE SAUCE. THIS IS A FIRM FAVOURITE WITH MY FAMILY.

ORZO AND CHICKEN BAKE

PASTICCIO DI ORZO E POLLO / SERVES 4—6

THIS IS AN OLD FAMILY FAVOURITE WITH THE LAYERS OF PASTA AND CHICKEN. ORZO IS A RICE-SHAPED PASTA THAT WORKS WELL IN CASSEROLES AND SOUPS. OR TRY THIS DISH WITH PENNE.

2 tbsp extra virgin olive oil

2 leeks, finely chopped

8 chicken thighs

1 garlic clove, finely chopped

400g orzo

2 potatoes, peeled and diced

100ml white wine

800ml chicken stock

200g green beans, sliced into 2cm lengths

4 tbsp cream

salt and freshly ground black pepper

4 tbsp freshly grated Parmesan

2 tbsp chopped parsley

1 Preheat the oven to 180°C/fan 160°C/gas 4.

2 Heat the olive oil in a casserole over a medium heat. Add the leeks and sauté for 4–5 minutes. Add the chicken and sauté on both sides until lightly golden. Add the garlic and cook for 2 minutes, then add the orzo and potatoes. Stir in the wine and bring to the boil. Simmer for 2 minutes, then add the chicken stock and bring to the boil.

3 Place the casserole in the oven and bake for 15–20 minutes, until the chicken is cooked through. Add the beans and cook for a further 5 minutes, then stir in the cream and season to taste. Sprinkle the top with the Parmesan and parsley and serve.

 KEEPING IT LOCAL: INSTEAD OF THE CHICKEN, I PLACE HADDOCK ON TOP AND ADD A LAYER OF HERB BREADCRUMBS, WHICH IS SCRUMPTIOUS.

RIGATONI ALLA VESUVIANA

SERVES 4

WITH A NAME LIKE THIS, DIRECT FROM VESUVIUS, IT CAN ONLY BE HOT AND FIERY! IT WILL WARM UP A WINTER EVENING.

350g rigatoni

extra virgin olive oil

2 garlic cloves, finely sliced

4 tomatoes, diced

2 red chillies, finely chopped

3 tbsp capers, drained

24 whole small black olives

2 tbsp sliced green olives

$1/2$ tsp salt

$1/2$ tsp caster sugar

freshly ground black pepper

2 tbsp chopped parsley

freshly grated Parmesan, to serve

cherry tomatoes on the vine, roasted

1 Cook the pasta according to the instructions on the package, retaining some of the cooking liquid.

2 Heat a generous amount of olive oil in a large frying pan over a low heat. Add the garlic and sauté for 1 minute, taking care that the garlic doesn't burn. Add the tomatoes, chillies, capers, olives, salt and sugar and simmer for 3–4 minutes. Season with freshly ground black pepper.

3 Add a little pasta cooking liquid to the sauce, then add the cooked, drained pasta. Toss and add the parsley, then sprinkle over the Parmesan. Place the roasted cherry tomatoes on top before serving.

KEEPING IT LOCAL: STIR IN SLICES OF BURREN SMOKEHOUSE HOT
SMOKED SALMON FOR A DELICIOUS ADDITION TO THIS DISH.

PAPPARDELLE WITH RAGÙ

PAPPARDELLE AL RAGÙ / SERVES 4

PERSONALLY, I LOVE THE SHREDDED SLOW-ROASTED PORK IN A RAGÙ, BUT MINCED BEEF IS EQUALLY GOOD. THE RAGÙ WILL FREEZE WELL AND IS IDEAL FOR ADDING TO ROASTED STUFFED RED PEPPERS AND EVEN TOPPED WITH SOME VERY THINLY SLICED POTATOES.

extra virgin olive oil

75g pancetta, diced

400g slow-roasted shoulder of pork, shredded

1 onion, finely chopped

1 carrot, finely diced

1 celery stalk, finely sliced

1 tsp dried oregano

2 garlic cloves, chopped

2 tbsp tomato purée

400g tinned chopped tomatoes

275ml beef stock

150ml red wine

salt and freshly ground black pepper

350g pappardelle

fresh basil leaves, to garnish

1 To make the ragù, heat a large saucepan with a little oil over a medium heat. Add the pancetta and cook until it's crispy and brown, then add the shredded pork.

2 Stir in the onion, carrot, celery and oregano and cook for about 5 minutes. Add the garlic and tomato purée and cook for 1 minute. Stir in the tinned tomatoes, stock, wine and some salt and freshly ground black pepper. Allow to simmer for 15–20 minutes, until a thick ragù has formed. Season to taste.

3 Meanwhile, cook the pasta according to the instructions on the package.

4 Add the cooked, drained pasta to the ragù sauce and garnish with basil leaves.

KEEPING IT LOCAL: USING KEPPLER'S APPLE CIDER INSTEAD OF THE WINE BRINGS A LOVELY ROUNDED FLAVOUR TO THE PORK RAGÙ. YOU COULD ALSO ADD 1 TSP CHOPPED THYME INSTEAD OF THE OREGANO.

LINGUINE WITH FENNEL AND PINE NUTS

LINGUINE CON FINOCCHI E PINOLI / SERVES 4

ADDING ANCHOVIES TO SAUCES ADDS RICHNESS AND A DEEP LAYER OF FLAVOUR. THE FIRST TIME I SERVED THIS TO MY CHILDREN, NERVOUS OF A BOYCOTT, I NEVER SAID THAT I HAD USED ANCHOVIES. TO THIS DAY, I JUST KEEP USING THEM AND THEY ARE NONE THE WISER! SOME COOKING SECRETS ARE SOMETIMES BEST KEPT TO YOURSELF.

extra virgin olive oil
2 medium onions, finely chopped
1 fennel bulb, finely chopped
3 garlic cloves, finely chopped
4 anchovies
100ml white wine
250g ripe tomatoes, deseeded and diced
freshly ground black pepper
350g linguine
4 tbsp pine nuts, lightly toasted
2 tbsp chopped fennel sprigs

1 To make the sauce, heat some olive oil in a large saucepan over a low heat. Add the onions and sauté for 7 minutes, until softened. Add the fennel and garlic and cook for 4–5 minutes. Add the anchovies and gently mash them with a wooden spoon so they dissolve in the oil and cook for 2 minutes. Add the white wine and simmer for 3–4 minutes. Stir in the tomatoes and simmer for 7–8 minutes. Season with freshly ground black pepper.
2 Cook the pasta according to the instructions on the package.
3 Stir the cooked, drained pasta into the sauce. Sprinkle with pine nuts and the chopped fennel sprigs. Drizzle with olive oil and serve.

KEEPING IT LOCAL: I FIND FENNEL GROWS VERY EASILY IN THE GARDEN, BUT I HAVE ALSO MADE THIS DISH WITH LEEKS INSTEAD OF FENNEL AND HAVE ADDED DILL FOR EXTRA FLAVOUR.

RICOTTA AND SPINACH LASAGNE ROLLS WITH TOMATO SAUCE

CANNELLONI DI RICOTTA E SPINACI CON SALSA DI POMODORO / SERVES 4

THIS RECIPE WILL SERIOUSLY IMPRESS YOUR FRIENDS. THERE ARE SO MANY FILLINGS TO CHOOSE FROM – SUNDRIED TOMATOES AND TAPENADE, WALNUTS, LEMON, ROSEMARY AND CREAM CHEESE OR EVEN A SALMON PÂTÉ ARE ALL DELICIOUS FILLING OPTIONS.

FOR THE TOMATO SAUCE:
extra virgin olive oil
1 garlic clove, finely chopped
1 tbsp sundried tomato purée
400g tinned plum tomatoes, crushed
1 tbsp chopped chives
sugar, to taste
salt and freshly ground black pepper

FOR THE PASTA DOUGH:
200g strong white flour
pinch of salt
2 eggs, beaten
1 tbsp extra virgin olive oil

FOR THE FILLING:
extra virgin olive oil
1 large leek, finely chopped
175g ricotta

450g baby spinach leaves
1 tsp chopped sage
1 tsp chopped parsley
$\frac{1}{2}$ tsp grated nutmeg
salt and freshly ground black pepper

FOR THE TOPPING:
75g breadcrumbs
50g freshly grated Parmesan

1 To prepare the sauce, heat some olive oil in a large pan over a low heat. Add the garlic and cook for about 2 minutes, until soft. Add the tomato purée and cook for a further minute. Add the tomatoes along with their juice, the chives and sugar to taste and season with salt and pepper. Bring to the boil, then reduce the heat and simmer for about 30 minutes, or until the sauce has thickened. Adjust the seasoning as required.

2 To make the pasta, sieve the flour and salt into a bowl. Pour in the beaten eggs and the oil and mix until the dough begins to come together. Turn out and knead until smooth. Wrap in plastic wrap and allow to rest in the fridge for at least 30 minutes.

3 To make the filling, heat some olive oil in a saucepan over a low heat. Add the leek and sauté for about 7 minutes, until softened but not brown. Allow to cool slightly, then add the ricotta. Stir in the spinach, sage, parsley and nutmeg and season to taste.

4 Roll out the pasta on a lightly floured surface until it measures about 20cm x 30cm.

5 Spread the ricotta and spinach filling over the pasta, leaving a clear border at the end. Roll it up and secure the edges with a little water. Wrap in plastic wrap and rest in the fridge for 30 minutes. Unwrap it and slice into 2cm-thick slices.

6 Preheat the oven to 180°C/fan 160°C/gas 4. Butter a large gratin dish.

7 Spoon some of the sauce on the base of the buttered gratin dish. Place the slices flat on the sauce and spoon over more sauce. Sprinkle over the breadcrumbs and Parmesan and bake for about 20 minutes, until golden.

 KEEPING IT LOCAL: BLEND ARDSALLAGH GOATS CHEESE WITH A GOOD CREAM CHEESE INSTEAD OF THE RICOTTA FOR A WONDERFUL FILLING FOR THE ROTOLINI.

BUCATINI WITH AUBERGINE AND TUNA

BUCATINI ALLE MELANZANE E TONNO / SERVES 4

AUBERGINE ADDS A SILKY TEXTURE TO SAUCES AND ABSORBS WONDERFUL FLAVOURS.

350g bucatini
extra virgin olive oil
2 aubergines, diced
2 garlic cloves, finely sliced
150g tinned tuna, drained
2 tbsp capers, drained and rinsed
1 1/2 tsp chopped fresh oregano or 1 tsp dried
5 tbsp grated Pecorino
salt and freshly ground black pepper
1 tbsp chopped parsley

1 Cook the bucatini according to the instructions on the package. Retain some of the cooking water.

2 Heat a generous amount of olive oil in a large saucepan over a medium heat. Add the diced aubergines and sauté for 5–6 minutes, stirring frequently, until lightly browned and softened. Add the garlic and cook for 1 minute. Stir in the tuna, capers and oregano and cook for about 5 minutes. Stir in half of the Pecorino.

3 Add the cooked, drained pasta to the sauce. You may need to add a little cooking liquid from the pasta if the sauce is too dry. Check for seasoning. Sprinkle the rest of the Pecorino over as well as the parsley and serve.

 KEEPING IT LOCAL: ADD LAYERS OF HOME-GROWN COURGETTE SLICES USING A VEGETABLE PEELER TO MAKE RIBBONS.

SEAFOOD LASAGNE

LASAGNA AI FRUTTI DI MARE / SERVES 6-8

THIS IS AN EASY VERSION OF THE TRADITIONAL LASAGNE. ALTERNATIVELY, YOU COULD JUST PREPARE THE SEAFOOD SAUCE AND USE FRESH PASTA. TRY THE FILLING WITH THE ROTOLINI ON PAGES 31–32.

60g butter

3 celery stalks, chopped

1 onion, chopped

4 tbsp flour

200ml cream

160ml milk

100ml white wine

½ lemon, zest and juice

salt and black freshly ground black pepper

300g white fish, diced

200g salmon, diced

9 lasagne sheets

225g prawns, shells removed

2 tbsp chopped dill

2 tbsp chopped parsley

4 tbsp breadcrumbs

1 Preheat the oven to 180°C/fan 160°C/gas 4. Butter a 20cm x 30cm gratin dish.

2 To prepare the sauce, heat the butter in a large saucepan over a low heat. Add the celery and onion and sauté for 7–8 minutes. Stir in the flour and cook for about 2 minutes, stirring all the time.

3 Add the cream, milk and wine and stir until the sauce thickens. Add the lemon zest and juice and season to taste. Add the white fish and salmon to the sauce and simmer on a low heat for 5–6 minutes, taking care not to stir.

4 Carefully spoon a layer of the sauce and fish on the base of the gratin dish. Add a layer of lasagne sheets, then some prawns, dill and parsley. Continue to layer, ending with the sauce and fish.

5 Sprinkle over the breadcrumbs and place in the oven for 20 minutes, until the lasagne is cooked through and the breadcrumbs are golden. Allow to stand for 5–10 minutes before serving.

 KEEPING IT LOCAL: SOMETIMES I MAKE A FISH PIE WITH A DIFFERENCE BY REPLACING THE LASAGNE WITH THINLY SLICED POTATOES – TRY THE AVONDALE VARIETY.

SPAGHETTI WITH ROAST TOMATOES AND SAGE

SPAGHETTI CON POMODORI AL FORNO E SALVIA / SERVES 4

THIS IS THE SIMPLEST OF RECIPES, SO THE QUALITY OF THE INGREDIENTS IS VERY IMPORTANT. IT'S A DISH THAT WAS MADE FOR ME BY ORETTA ZANINI DE VITA, AUTHOR OF *THE ENCYCLOPAEDIA OF PASTA*, IN HER HOME IN ROME. I REALLY LIKE THE FRESHNESS OF THIS DISH AND IT'S DELICIOUS FOR LUNCH.

250g cherry tomatoes

3 garlic cloves, halved

3–4 large sage leaves or 6–8 small leaves, finely sliced, plus a few to garnish

5 tbsp extra virgin olive oil

salt and freshly ground black pepper

350g spaghetti

100g goats cheese

1 Preheat the oven to 180°C/fan 160°C/gas 4.
2 Place the cherry tomatoes, garlic and sage leaves in a roasting pan and drizzle with the olive oil. Season with salt and freshly ground black pepper. Roast for 10–12 minutes, stirring from time to time, until the tomatoes are softened and lightly caramelised.
3 Meanwhile, cook the spaghetti according to the instructions on the package.
4 Drain the pasta, then mix with the roast tomato sauce. Sprinkle over the goats cheese and garnish with sage leaves.

  KEEPING IT LOCAL: SPRINKLE WITH A SEMI-SOFT DUBARRA CHEESE. THE PEPPER ONE IS SUPERB WITH THE ROASTED TOMATOES IN THIS DISH. YOU CAN ALSO ADD ROASTED YELLOW PEPPERS IN THE SUMMER.

LIGURIAN PASTA WITH PESTO AND GREEN BEANS

TROFIE AL PESTO E FAGIOLINI / SERVES 4–6

TROFIE IS A LIGURIAN PASTA MADE FROM WATER AND FLOUR – NO EGG IS ADDED. THE SECRET OF THIS DISH IS THE PESTO, THOUGH OF COURSE I WOULD ALSO SAY IT'S THE POTATOES! ADD BEANS AND PEAS WITH THINLY SLICED FENNEL FOR A DELICIOUS SUPPER.

350g trofie (see recipe below)

3 medium potatoes, peeled and diced small

100g green beans, trimmed and cut into 4cm lengths

120g basil pesto (see page 75)

freshly ground black pepper

4–5 tbsp freshly grated Parmesan

1 Cook the trofie in a pot of salted boiling water for 6 minutes, until it's just slightly undercooked. Add the potatoes to the trofie and cook for 3 minutes. Add the beans and cook for 2 minutes.

2 Drain the trofie, potatoes and beans, retaining a little of the cooking liquid. Return everything back to the saucepan and stir in the pesto, loosening with a little of the retained cooking liquid as required. Season with freshly ground black pepper.

3 Spoon into a serving bowl, sprinkle with Parmesan and serve.

TROFIE

350g strong white flour   1 tsp salt   150ml water

1 Mix the flour and salt in a bowl. Add just enough water to form a soft dough. Place the dough on a floured surface and knead very well, until the dough is smooth.

2 Roll the dough out until it's 2cm thick, then cut it into 2cm pieces. Using your fingertips, roll the pieces on a floured surface until they're about 4cm long. Flour your hands, then using the palm of one hand and 2 fingers of your other hand, roll the pasta to form long squiggly lengths. Place on a floured tray ready for cooking.

KEEPING IT LOCAL: WELL, IF POTATOES AND PASTA WEREN'T LOCAL ENOUGH, HOW ABOUT TRYING NETTLE PESTO? USE THICK GARDENING GLOVES TO PICK THE NETTLES AND DON'T FORGET TO WASH THEM!

ROAST PUMPKIN AND RED PEPPER CANNELLONI

CANNELLONI CON ZUCCA E PEPERONI / SERVES 6

A DELICIOUS VEGETARIAN OPTION, THIS RECIPE MAY SEEM LONG BUT IT IS WELL WORTH THE TIME SPENT. IF YOU DON'T HAVE CANNELLONI TUBES, JUST USE ROLLED-UP PARCOOKED LASAGNE SHEETS.

extra virgin olive oil

150g pumpkin, peeled and diced

2 onions, finely chopped

2 garlic cloves, finely chopped

400g baby spinach

1 jar roasted red peppers, drained and chopped

250g ricotta cheese

freshly grated nutmeg

salt and freshly ground black pepper

knob of butter, melted

16 cannelloni tubes

100g freshly grated Parmesan

4 tbsp breadcrumbs

FOR THE SAUCE:

80g butter

80g plain flour

650ml milk (or use half vegetable stock and half milk)

salt and freshly ground black pepper

1 Preheat the oven to 180°C/fan 160°C/gas 4.

2 For the filling, heat some oil in a saucepan over a low heat and sauté the pumpkin and onions until soft. Add the garlic and cook for a further 2 minutes. Remove from the pan and set aside in a large bowl.

3 Add the spinach to the pan and allow it to wilt, which will take 1 or 2 minutes. Place the spinach in a colander and allow it to drain.

4 Add the drained spinach to the pumpkin and garlic, followed by the red peppers and ricotta, and mix well. Grate a little nutmeg over the mixture and check for seasoning.

5 To make the sauce, combine the butter and flour in a saucepan and cook, stirring over a low heat, for 4–5 minutes. Add the milk and whisk continuously until it's almost boiling. Reduce the heat and simmer for a further 3–4 minutes, stirring often. Season to taste and set aside.

6 Brush an ovenproof dish with the melted butter and spread a little of the white sauce in the base of the dish.

7 Fill the cannelloni tubes with the mixture filling using a piping bag. Layer the tubes in the dish and pour over the rest of the white sauce. Sprinkle over the Parmesan and breadcrumbs. Bake for 20–25 minutes, until golden. Allow to stand for 5–10 minutes and serve.

KEEPING IT LOCAL: COMBINE JANET'S COUNTRY FAYRE BEETROOT BLUSH RELISH WITH CREAM AND SPINACH FOR A CANNELLONI STUFFING.

PANCETTA AND PESTO RISOTTO

RISOTTO CON PANCETTA E PESTO / SERVES 4–6

THIS IS A GREAT WAY TO USE UP LEFTOVER PESTO. SUNDRIED TOMATO PESTO, ROCKET PESTO OR ROASTED RED PEPPER PESTO WILL ADD EXTRA FLAVOUR TO THE RISOTTO.

2 tbsp extra virgin olive oil
knob of butter
2 leeks, finely sliced
4 slices pancetta, chopped
2 garlic cloves, chopped
400g risotto rice
150ml white wine
1.4 litres chicken stock, heated to simmering
6 tbsp basil pesto (see page 75)
2 tbsp freshly grated Parmesan
salt and freshly ground black pepper
fresh basil leaves, to garnish

1 Heat a large, heavy-based saucepan over a medium heat and add the oil and a knob of butter. When the butter is foaming, add the leeks and cook for 5 minutes, until it begins to soften. Add the pancetta and cook for 2 minutes. Add the garlic and rice and cook for a few minutes, until the rice is shiny and opaque. Add the wine and simmer for 1 minute, stirring constantly.
2 Reduce the heat and add the stock a ladleful at a time, stirring constantly, until each ladleful is absorbed into the rice. The rice should be creamy but firm to the bite. Stir in the pesto.
3 Remove from the heat and stir in the Parmesan, then season to taste and garnish with basil leaves.

 KEEPING IT LOCAL: OMIT THE PANCETTA AND STIR A TABLESPOON OF ED HICK'S DELICIOUS AND VERY UNUSUAL BACON JAM THROUGH THE RISOTTO.

OVEN-BAKED MUSHROOM RISOTTO

RISOTTO AI FUNGHI AL FORNO / SERVES 4

MUSHROOM PICKING IS BECOMING A BIT OF A PASTIME IN IRELAND NOWADAYS, BUT WHEN I WAS GROWING UP, IT WAS PART OF OUR AUTUMNAL LIFE. AS CHILDREN, WE WERE GIVEN BOWLS AND TOLD TO GO FORTH AND PICK. HEAVEN KNOWS WHAT I USED TO BRING HOME – I PICKED EVERYTHING. LUCKILY, MY MOTHER KNEW WHAT WAS SAFE TO COOK.

extra virgin olive oil

200g mushrooms, sliced

2 garlic cloves, finely sliced

1 onion, chopped

300g risotto rice

2 celery stalks, finely sliced

3 tbsp chopped parsley

1 tbsp chopped thyme

750ml chicken stock

150ml dry white wine

100ml cream

salt and freshly ground black pepper

Parmesan shavings, to serve

1 Preheat the oven to 180°C/fan 160°C/gas 4.

2 Heat some oil in a casserole dish over a medium heat. Add the mushrooms and garlic and sauté for 2–3 minutes, until just cooked. Remove from the pan and set aside.

3 Add the onion and sauté on a low heat for 7–10 minutes, until light golden. Add the rice, celery, parsley and thyme. Allow to cook for 2 minutes, stirring from time to time.

4 In a separate pan, heat the chicken stock, then add the wine and stock to the casserole dish. Stir and cover tightly with foil or a lid.

5 Place in the oven and cook for approximately 40 minutes, stirring occasionally, until the liquid has been absorbed and the rice is just tender. Remove from the oven, add the mushroom and garlic mixture and stir in the cream. Season to taste. Drizzle with some olive oil and sprinkle with Parmesan shavings.

KEEPING IT LOCAL: GARDEN-GROWN BEETROOT, ROASTED, HAS A DISTINCTIVE SWEET AND EARTHY FLAVOUR INSTEAD OF THE MUSHROOMS.

ASPARAGUS AND PEAR RISOTTO

RISOTTO CON ASPARAGI E PERE / SERVES 4-6

YOU MAY HAVE THE INITIAL REACTION THAT I HAD WHEN I SAW THIS DISH ON A MENU IN FLORENCE FOR THE FIRST TIME – WILL IT WORK? WELL, OF COURSE I HAD TO TRY IT, AND LET ME SAY IT WORKS JUST BEAUTIFULLY.

2 pears, sliced
30g butter
2 tbsp extra virgin olive oil
1 onion, finely chopped
1 large garlic clove, sliced
400g risotto rice
150ml white wine
1.5 litres chicken stock, heated to simmering
16 asparagus spears, sliced lengthways and blanched
75g soft goats cheese
salt and freshly ground black pepper

1 Sauté the pears in the butter on a medium-low heat, until lightly browned on both sides. Set aside to put in at the end (or chargrill the pears for visual impact).
2 Heat the oil over a low heat in a large heavy-based saucepan. Add the onion and cook for 8 minutes, until it's beginning to soften. Add the garlic and rice and cook for a few minutes, until the rice is shiny and opaque. Add the wine and simmer for 1 minute, stirring constantly. Add the stock a ladleful at a time, stirring constantly, until each ladleful is absorbed. Add the pears with the last ladle of stock. The rice should be creamy but firm to the bite.
3 Add the blanched asparagus spears and heat through. Remove from the heat and stir in the goats cheese. Season to taste and serve.

KEEPING IT LOCAL: STIR IN BULMER'S PEAR CIDER INSTEAD OF THE WHITE WINE FOR A VERY PLEASANT AND SWEET RISOTTO.

POLENTA GNOCCHI WITH BASIL PESTO

GNOCCHI DI POLENTA CON PESTO / SERVES 4

THIS IS AN EASY AND VERY IMPRESSIVE STARTER. THE CHILDREN CAN HELP — IT'S ALWAYS GOOD TO HAVE AN EXTRA PAIR OF HELPING HANDS WHEN PREPARING FOR A DINNER PARTY.

750ml water

1 tsp salt

200g polenta (cornmeal), quick cook variety

75g butter

50g freshly grated Parmesan

salt and freshly ground black pepper

extra virgin olive oil

5 tbsp basil pesto (see page 75)

pine nuts, to garnish

1 Brush a 20cm x 30cm baking pan with olive oil.
2 Pour the water and salt into a large heavy-based saucepan and bring to the boil. Gradually pour in the polenta while whisking continuously and quickly to ensure the mixture stays smooth and no lumps form. Add in the butter and Parmesan.
3 Reduce the heat to its lowest setting and cook for 1–2 minutes, until the mixture is thick and creamy and coming away from the pan (add more water if necessary). Season to taste.
4 Pour the polenta into the oiled baking pan, smooth the surface and cover lightly with parchment paper. Cool quickly, then place in the fridge to set for 5 hours.
5 For polenta shapes, cut out stars using a cookie cutter. Heat some olive oil in a large frying pan over a medium heat and sauté on both sides until golden. Keep warm and pile on top of each other. Drizzle over the basil pesto and garnish with pine nuts.

 KEEPING IT LOCAL: REPLACE THE PESTO WITH A CHEESE SAUCE USING THE NUTTY-FLAVOURED HARD-STYLE KNOCKDRINNA GOLD GOATS CHEESE AND CHOPPED WALNUTS.

COUSCOUS WITH SAFFRO

COUSCOUS ALLO ZAFFERANO / SERVES 4-6

THE CARAWAY SEEDS GIVE A DIFFERENT ANGLE TO THE COUSCOUS, BUT IF THEY'RE NOT YOUR FAVOURITE, ADD CHOPPED ROSEMARY OR DILL.

425ml vegetable stock
pinch of saffron
200g couscous
1 lemon, zest of 1 and juice of $^1/_2$
extra virgin olive oil
1 medium aubergine, diced
1 red pepper, diced
1 yellow pepper, diced
1 courgette, thinly sliced
1 tsp caraway seeds
2 garlic cloves, finely sliced
1 green chilli, finely chopped
salt and freshly ground black pepper

1 Heat the stock with the saffron in a large saucepan. Bring to the boil and remove from the heat. Place the couscous into a large bowl and pour the hot stock over the couscous, followed by a good glug of olive oil. Stir in the lemon zest and juice, mix well and set aside for 3–4 minutes, until the grains have swelled and absorbed all the liquid. Cover to keep warm.

2 In the meantime, heat some oil in a large frying pan over a medium heat. Add the aubergine and sauté for 3–4 minutes, until lightly golden. Stir in the red and yellow peppers, courgette slices and caraway seeds and sauté for 3–4 minutes. Add the garlic and chilli and cook for 1 minute.

3 Use a fork to fluff up the couscous and stir in the vegetables. Season to taste and serve as a side dish to fish or chicken.

KEEPING IT LOCAL: STIR IN GARDEN ROCKET AND OLD MACDONNELL'S GOATS CHEESE FOR A LOVELY SUMMER SALAD.

FARRO AND TOMATO SALAD

INSALATA DI FARRO E POMODORO / SERVES 4

FARRO IS A HULLED WHEAT GRAIN THAT HAS A NUTTY TASTE AND A LOVELY BITE. IT'S AN ANCIENT SUPERFOOD AND RUSTIC STAPLE WHICH IS WELL WORTH ADDING TO OUR STORE CUPBOARD. BARLEY OR COUSCOUS ALSO WORK WELL IN THIS RECIPE – JUST COOK ACCORDING TO THE PACKAGE INSTRUCTIONS.

250g farro
$\frac{1}{2}$ tsp salt
3 tomatoes, skinned and diced
1 red onion, finely chopped
2 tbsp chopped chives
flat-leaf parsley, to garnish

FOR THE VINAIGRETTE:
100ml extra virgin olive oil
3 tbsp balsamic vinegar
1 garlic clove, sliced
salt and freshly ground black pepper

1 Add 1 litre of water to a large saucepan, then pour in the farro and salt. Bring to the boil and simmer for about 30 minutes, until the farro is tender. Drain well and transfer to a bowl to cool.
2 Meanwhile, combine the tomatoes, onion and chives together. Set aside.
3 Whisk all the vinaigrette ingredients together in a bowl.
4 Place the farro in a large serving bowl. Add the tomato mixture and pour over most of the vinaigrette. For maximum flavour, leave to infuse for at least 5 hours. Season to taste. Mix again, sprinkle over the parsley and serve.

KEEPING IT LOCAL: FOR AN AUTUMNAL TWIST, FRY OFF SOME LOCAL MUSHROOMS WITH GARLIC TO REPLACE THE TOMATOES.

PARMESAN POLENTA CHIPS

PATATINE DI POLENTA CON PARMIGIANO / SERVES 4

WE ALL LOVE CHIPS – THEY'RE COMFORT FOOD AT ITS BEST. FOR CHIPS WITH A DIFFERENCE, POLENTA IS SO VERSATILE AND MAKES REALLY NICE CHIPS AND IT'S A GREAT CHANGE FROM POTATO WEDGES.

extra virgin olive oil
750ml water
1 tsp salt
200g polenta (cornmeal), quick cook variety
75g butter
50g freshly grated Parmesan
salt and freshly ground black pepper
1 egg, beaten
3 tbsp polenta

1 Brush a 20cm x 30cm baking pan with olive oil.
2 Pour the water and salt into a large heavy-based saucepan and bring to the boil. Gradually pour in the polenta while whisking continuously and quickly to ensure the mixture stays smooth and no lumps form. Add in the butter and Parmesan.
3 Reduce the heat to its lowest setting and cook for 1–2 minutes, until the mixture is thick and creamy and coming away from the edge of the pan (add more water if necessary). Season to taste.
4 Pour the polenta into the oiled baking pan, smooth the surface and cover with parchment paper. Cool quickly and place in the fridge to set for 5 hours.
5 Turn the polenta onto a clean surface. Using a sharp knife, slice lengthways into 2cm-wide strips and cut the strips into 7cm lengths.
6 Place the beaten egg and 3 tbsp polenta in separate shallow bowls. Heat some olive oil in a large frying pan over a medium heat. Dip each strip into the beaten egg and then the polenta, then fry on both sides until golden. Keep warm in the oven until ready to serve.

 KEEPING IT LOCAL: DID YOU KNOW THAT POLENTA, OR CORNMEAL, WAS ALSO KNOWN AS YELLOW MEAL AND WAS USED FOR BREAD AND AS AN ALTERNATIVE TO POTATOES IN IRELAND IN THE 1800S?

FRUIT

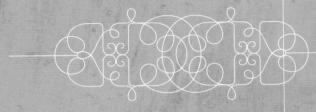

HAVING BEEN BROUGHT UP ON A FARM IN WICKLOW WITH A WONDERFUL MOTHER WHO LOVED TO COOK, I WAS ACCUSTOMED TO A SUBSTANTIAL DESSERT TO FINISH A MEAL, AND THE SWEETER AND MORE CHOCOLATEY IT WAS, THE BETTER!

SO IMAGINE MY SURPRISE WHEN ON MY FIRST VISIT TO SICILY, IN A VERY POSH RESTAURANT IN THE NORMAN TOWN OF ERICE, I ASKED FOR DESSERT AND WAS HANDED AN ORANGE, BEAUTIFULLY PERCHED ON A PLATE WITH A SHARP KNIFE ALONGSIDE. I RAISED AN EYEBROW AND WAS HASTILY OFFERED GRAPES AS WELL. NO GOOEY CHOCOLATE?

BUT THE FRUIT TRULY WAS A DELICIOUS END TO MY AMAZING MEAL OF SMOKED CARPACCIO OF TUNA FOLLOWED BY SEAFOOD COUSCOUS. ISN'T IT INTERESTING HOW MEMORIES OF EVENTS AND CONVERSATIONS COME FLOODING BACK WHEN YOU RECALL THE FOOD YOU ENJOYED AT THE TIME?

HERE ARE SOME OF MY FAVOURITE ITALIAN FRUITS.

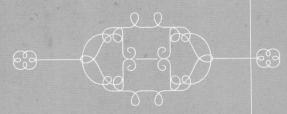

LEMONS

Who can resist the iconic fruit of Sorrento and the Amalfi coast, packed with intense flavour and great health properties? As you drive along, terrace groves of lemons dripping from the trees pass by. The intense flavour gets stronger and by July or August they are at their best. The skins have an abundance of oils, ideal for the preparation of limoncello. Around the world, chefs wax lyrical about the Amalfi lemons, but the Sicilians beg to differ as they are equally, if not more, proud of their lemon gold.

When I think of lemons, my mind goes to the weird-looking *cedro*, or citron as it's known in English. I picked it up at a market in Palermo. It looks like an ugly lemon but is more fragrant and drier. One of Claudio's cousins made a fabulous jam with it. I have since heard that the cedro is great for keeping moths away!

ORANGES

I have often spoken about the oranges of Sicily and the Conca d'Oro (Valley of Gold) as you drive into Palermo. It's a fantastic sight, especially from the hills above, looking down on the golden oranges that light up the route into this beautiful city.

A bit more exciting is the Battle of the Oranges in Ivrea, near Turin, which takes place in February each year. The Carnevale d'Ivrea dates back to the Middle Ages, when beans were used, thrown by the poor at the feudal lords. Sometime within the last hundred years oranges began to be used instead, first thrown by young girls from their balconies to get the attention of the boys! Now no one gets to leave untouched by pulp.

It's difficult to know just when oranges were introduced into what is now Italy. The Romans knew of them from their travels to the southern and eastern reaches of their empire and oranges are occasionally depicted in Roman art. However, it's generally accepted as fact that citrus fruits (oranges, lemons, citron) were first cultivated in Sicily during the Arab period in the ninth and tenth centuries. Indeed, the modern English word 'orange', like the Italian 'Arancia', probably derives from the Arabic 'Naranj'.

FIGS

Although dried figs are available throughout the year, there is nothing nicer than the unique taste of a fresh fig. Would you believe that they're a member of the mulberry family? Lusciously sweet, they have a complex texture that combines the slight chewiness of their flesh, the smooth silkiness of their skin and the crunchiness of their seeds. Since fresh figs are quick to perish, they should only be picked or purchased a day or two in advance.

While at the market during my very first year visiting Italy, Claudio kept me enthralled about *Figi d'Indi* (figs of India). He described in detail the lusciousness of the sweet fruit. I was surprised to see that they don't resemble a fig whatsoever – in fact, they're the fruit of the cactus plant. His description was perfect as I bit into one juicy, messy and deliciously sweet fruit. I can't imagine Sicily without them now and if you have the chance to try one, remember that only tourists spit out the pips!

Here at Ballyknocken, we were so proud of ourselves last year when we harvested three very good-looking figs! Hopefully this year we will have a 100% increase on that production.

FRESH FRUIT TART (SEE P.179)

SUMMER BERRIES WITH MAPLE ZABAGLIONE

BACCHE ESTIVE CON ZABAGLIONE / SERVES 4-6

MAPLE SYRUP ISN'T TRADITIONAL, BUT I LOVE IT IN ZABAGLIONE. THIS IS A CLASSIC AND IS OFTEN SERVED WITH RIPE, JUICY, SWEET PEACHES, WHICH ARE PACKED WITH THE SUNSHINE GOODNESS OF VITAMIN D.

4 egg yolks
100ml maple syrup
1 tsp almond extract
500g fresh strawberries, blueberries, blackberries and/or raspberries, washed and trimmed
3 tbsp flaked almonds, toasted, to decorate (optional)
mint leaves or borage flowers, to decorate

1 Combine the egg yolks, maple syrup and almond extract in a bain marie (a heatproof bowl set over a pot of simmering water) and whisk with an electric beater until it has more than doubled in volume and the eggs have cooked, which will probably take about 7 minutes.
2 Arrange a selection of berries into small glasses, serving bowls or espresso cups and spoon over the maple zabaglione.
3 Sprinkle the flaked almonds over the zabaglione and decorate with mint leaves or borage flowers.

KEEPING IT LOCAL: OUR CLIMATE PRODUCES THE MOST DELICIOUS PLUMS, WHICH, WHEN ROASTED AND CARAMELISED, ARE WONDERFUL WITH THE ZABAGLIONE.

FRESH FIG ICE CREAM

GELATO DI FICHI / MAKES ABOUT 600ML

A LITTLE INDULGENCE AND A LOT OF FRESH FRUIT! THIS IS LESS ICE CREAM AND MORE FIGS, SO IT IS DEFINITELY IN THE HEALTHY CATEGORY!

12 ripe figs, trimmed
160g vanilla sugar (see below)
1 lemon, zest only
200ml double cream, lightly whipped
figs or blackberries, to serve

1 Place the figs, sugar and lemon zest in a food processor and blend until smooth. Fold in the whipped cream.
2 Pour into a container and freeze for 2 hours. Then, using an electric beater, whisk the mixture. Repeat this three times, refreezing for 1 hour after each time. Allow to set overnight.
3 Before serving, place in the fridge for 30 minutes to soften. Spoon into glasses and serve with fresh figs or blackberries.

KEEPING IT LOCAL: REPLACE THE LEMON WITH LAVENDER. TO MAKE YOUR OWN VANILLA SUGAR, YOU WILL NEED 1 VANILLA POD, DESEEDED, AND 500G CASTER SUGAR. PLACE THE SUGAR IN AN AIRTIGHT JAR AND ADD IN THE VANILLA POD AND IT WILL BE READY TO USE IN 3-4 DAYS. I DOUBT THAT YOU WILL KEEP IT FOR LONG!

FRUIT GRANITA

GRANITA DI FRUTTA / SERVES ABOUT 4–6 IN SMALL GLASSES

THERE ARE SO MANY DIFFERENT COMBINATIONS FOR GRANITA, SO I FOUND IT BEST TO HAVE A BASIC STANDARD
RECIPE AND EXPERIMENT A LITTLE. AN IMPORTANT POINT TO REMEMBER IS TO MAKE IT VERY SWEET AND FRUITY,
BECAUSE WHEN FROZEN, THE FLAVOUR IS FAR LESS INTENSE.

600g fruit

150g caster sugar

350ml water

1 lemon, zest and juice

mint leaves, to decorate

1 Prepare the fruit by peeling, destoning or deseeding it, then roughly chopping it. Place
   the prepared fruit in a blender and process until smooth. Sieve the fruit into a bowl.
2 In the meantime, combine the sugar, water, lemon zest and juice in a saucepan and bring
   to the boil. Simmer until a thick syrup begins to form. Allow to cool.
3 Combine the sugar syrup with the fruit purée. Pour into a container and cover with a lid.
   Freeze for 4 hours or until crystals form. Using a fork, roughly break up the crystals or
   pulse in a food processor. Refreeze and repeat this three times, refreezing for 1 hour each
   time.
4 Spoon into serving glasses and decorate with mint leaves or slices of the fruit that you
   have used.

Some combinations to try:
- WATERMELON AND PEACH: Equal quantities of watermelon and peaches.
- HONEYDEW MELON AND STEM GINGER: 5 small pieces of stem ginger and 600g
  honeydew melon.
- RED GRAPES AND CANTALOUPE MELON: 300g seedless red grapes and 300g
  cantaloupe melon.
- PEACH AND ORANGE: Equal quantities of peaches and oranges and the zest of 1
  lemon.
- MANGO, MINT AND STRAWBERRY: 3 ripe mangoes, 3 mint sprigs and 400g
  strawberries.

 KEEPING IT LOCAL: IN THE AUTUMN, I MAKE AN APPLE AND WHISKEY GRANITA USING THE APPLES
FROM OUR ORCHARD. IT'S DELICIOUS AS A PALATE CLEANSER, BUT GO EASY ON THE WHISKEY!

PLUM AND CHIANTI COMPOTE WITH GINGER

PRUGNE AL CHIANTI E ZENZERO / SERVES 4

THIS IS A WONDERFULLY SIMPLE DESSERT THAT CAN BE MADE WELL AHEAD OF TIME, AND THE GINGER ADDS A LOVELY BITE.

1 ½ kg plums, halved and pitted
200g caster sugar
500ml Chianti
100ml water
2 pieces of stem ginger, chopped, plus extra to decorate
1 orange, zest only
½ lemon, zest and juice
1 cinnamon stick
3 tbsp orangecello or Grand Marnier
crème fraîche, to serve

1 Combine the plums, sugar, Chianti, water, ginger, orange and lemon zest and cinnamon stick in a large saucepan. Bring to the boil, then reduce the heat and gently simmer for 12–15 minutes.
2 Remove the cinnamon stick, then place three-quarters of the poached plums and all of the liquid into a blender and process until smooth. Pour into a large bowl.
3 Add the lemon juice and orangecello and stir well, then add the remaining plums. Ladle into serving bowls, sprinkle over some ginger and serve with crème fraîche.

KEEPING IT LOCAL: REPLACE THE CHIANTI WITH SOME GOOD LOCAL CIDER AND A SPRIG OF ROSEMARY FROM THE GARDEN.

ROASTED RHUBARB AND STRAWBERRIES WITH BASIL SYRUP

RABARBARO ARROSTO E FRAGOLE CON SCIROPPO DI BASILICO / SERVES 4

THIS IS MY IRISH-ITALIAN COMBO. ROASTING THE FRUIT GIVES YOU PLENTY OF TIME TO GET ON WITH OTHER ACTIVITIES AND IT HELPS THE RHUBARB HOLD ITS SHAPE AND COLOUR.

8 medium-large rhubarb stalks, washed and trimmed, sliced into 5cm lengths on the diagonal
75g caster sugar
4 tbsp fresh orange juice
300g strawberries, washed, hulled and sliced in half

FOR THE BASIL SYRUP:

60g caster sugar
50ml water
1 tsp vanilla extract
20 fresh basil leaves

1 Preheat the oven to 180°C/fan 160°C/gas 4.
2 Place the rhubarb in a roasting pan and sprinkle over the sugar and orange juice. Place in the oven to roast for about 15 minutes, or until the fruit is just cooked. Allow to cool.
3 In the meantime, to make the syrup, place the sugar, water and vanilla in a small saucepan. Heat until the sugar has dissolved and simmer until a syrup has formed. Allow to cool.
4 Place the basil leaves in a food processor with the cooled syrup and blend until smooth.
5 Arrange the rhubarb on a serving platter. Sprinkle the strawberries over and drizzle with the basil syrup.

KEEPING IT LOCAL: I HAVE ALSO MADE THIS WITH PEARS AND BLUEBERRIES FROM MY GARDEN WITH FANTASTIC RESULTS. THIS IS ALSO DELICIOUS SERVED WITH WICKLOW BLUE CHEESE.

POACHED NECTARINE, PEACH AND FIG SALAD WITH LEMON AND PISTACHIOS

PESCHENOCI, PESCHE E FICHI COTTI CON LIMONE E PISTACCHI / SERVES 4-6

IF I HAVE ANY POACHED FRUIT LEFT I LIKE TO LAYER THE FRUITS, ESPECIALLY THE FIGS, IN A GLASS SERVING BOWL WITH YOGHURT AND SESAME BISCUITS IN BETWEEN.

5 figs, halved

3 peaches, halved and pitted

3 nectarines, pitted and sliced in wedges

3 tbsp pistachios, to decorate

mint leaves, to decorate

FOR THE SYRUP:

200g caster sugar

300ml white wine

200ml water

3-4 cardamom pods, lightly crushed

1 lemon, zest and juice

1 To make the syrup, place the sugar, white wine, water, cardamom pods, lemon zest and juice in a saucepan. Bring to the boil, then reduce the heat and gently simmer for 8–10 minutes, until a syrup forms.

2 Carefully place the fruit into the syrup and poach lightly for 4–5 minutes. Remove from the heat and allow to cool.

3 Using a slotted spoon, place the fruit onto a serving platter or bowl. Remove the cardamom pods from the syrup, then drizzle the syrup over the fruit. Sprinkle with pistachios and mint leaves.

 KEEPING IT LOCAL: THERE ARE SO MANY FARMHOUSE ICE CREAMS AVAILABLE AND I PARTICULARLY ENJOY THIS WITH A VANILLA FLAVOUR. HOW ABOUT REPLACING THE PEACHES AND NECTARINES WITH STRAWBERRIES AND LOGANBERRIES?

ORANGE AND MELON SALAD WITH RASPBERRY SAUCE

MACEDONIA DI ARANCIA E MELONE CON SALSA DI LAMPONI / SERVES 4

THERE IS NOTHING NICER THAN A LIGHT FRESH FRUIT DESSERT AFTER A LENGTHY MEAL. TRY WARMING THE ORANGE SEGMENTS FOR A WINTER DESSERT OR EVEN SERVE WITH POACHED PEARS.

3 oranges, peeled and segmented

1 bunch red seedless grapes, washed and stemmed

½ cantaloupe melon, peeled and sliced into thin wedges or ribbons

FOR THE SAUCE:

200g raspberries, washed

5 tbsp icing sugar

½ orange, zest only

1 To make the sauce, place the raspberries, icing sugar and orange zest in a blender and process until smooth. Sieve to remove the raspberry seeds.

2 Arrange the orange segments, grapes and melon wedges in rows on a large serving platter and drizzle the raspberry sauce across.

KEEPING IT LOCAL: MAKE THIS A WONDERFUL FINISH TO A MEAL BY SERVING ARTISAN CHEESES ALONGSIDE, ESPECIALLY A SOFT GOATS CHEESE SUCH AS THE DELICIOUS ARDRAHAN.

NUTS, BEANS & LEGUMES

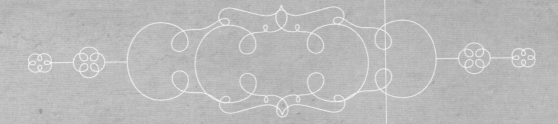

NUTS, BEANS AND LEGUMES WERE CERTAINLY NOT PART
OF MY DAILY DIET WHEN GROWING UP IN WICKLOW. EVEN
THOUGH BEANS AND LEGUMES IN PARTICULAR GROW
WELL IN THE IRISH CLIMATE, THEY JUST DIDN'T SEEM TO
BE AS POPULAR AS THE TRADITIONAL STAPLES.

ON ONE OF OUR TRIPS TO ITALY, CLAUDIO TOOK ME TO
A TINY RESTAURANT IN THE HILLS OF TUSCANY AND
RAVED IN ADVANCE ABOUT THE BEAN SALAD – HONESTLY,
I SECRETLY THOUGHT THAT I WASN'T TRAVELLING ALL
THIS WAY TO EAT EITHER BEANS OR A SALAD. I CAN
NOW ADMIT THAT IT WAS THE HIGHLIGHT OF THE MEAL
FOR ME. I'LL NEVER FORGET THE SIMPLICITY OF THAT
WARM CANNELLINI BEAN SALAD – BEANS DRESSED WITH
LEMON JUICE, OLIVE OIL, FLAT-LEAF PARSLEY, SALT AND
PEPPER MADE A TRIUMPHANT ENTRY THAT DAY ONTO MY
LIST OF FAVOURITES.

NUTS

Pistachios, walnuts, almonds, pine nuts and hazelnuts appear frequently in the Mediterranean diet. They're used to make pesto, served with salads and added to sauces, and just when you think you can't eat another nut, then you can tuck into pistachio ice cream or sip frangelico or amaretto.

Nuts bring a wonderful texture and depth of flavour to dishes. Most people think of nuts only for their calorific and fat content, but they are also full of fibre, vitamin E, selenium and omega 3 and are a good antioxidant.

Throughout Italy, everyone starts to make nocino on 24 June, which is St John's Day (Giovanni's Day), when tradition has it that the walnuts must be picked on this day. Nocino is a dark-coloured liqueur with a hint of spice (see page 198). It has a 35% alcohol content, so a little goes a long way. I like to add it into desserts or in the filling for special cakes, but best of all it's delicious over vanilla ice cream on a summer's day.

BEANS AND LEGUMES

Beans and legumes are one of the world's most valuable foods. Rich in fibre, they also reduce serum cholesterol levels. All Italian mamas believe that beans are essential for optimal health and should be included in the diet as often as possible. In fact, most households in Italy would have beans incorporated in one or two meals a week.

Cannellini beans are perhaps the most popular and they are simply referred to as *fagioli*. Other popular beans from central Italy are corona, soranin and toscanello. While Italians will substitute one white bean for another, each variety provides its own shape and texture to the dishes that they're in.

Borlotti beans hail from the north and they are considered to be the healthiest due to the high concentration of iron. The bean is popular as a meat substitute and also adds creaminess to a recipe. We've been very successful in growing them here in the garden at my cookery school. I love to pick them and straight away steam them slightly, add sautéed chopped chilli and a drizzle of lemon juice for lunch.

Fava beans (also known as broad beans), either fresh or dried, are the staple of Abruzzo, Puglia and Campania. As the beans are fairly hardy it's best to buy them already split and skinned, otherwise they take several hours to cook.

BEAN SOUP

ZUPPA DI FAGIOLI / SERVES 4

THE ITALIAN EQUIVALENT TO CHICKEN SOUP - *ZUPPA DI FAGIOLI* IS GOOD FOR THE SOUL. THIS IS MY YUMMY VERSION, WHICH IS A GOOD COMFORTING SOUP WHEN YOU NEED A PICK-ME-UP.

150g dried cannellini beans

100g dried borlotti beans

extra virgin olive oil

100g pancetta, diced

2 carrots, diced

2 celery stalks, trimmed and sliced

1 large leek, finely sliced on the diagonal

2 garlic cloves, finely sliced

2 bay leaves

2 tsp finely chopped fresh oregano (or 1 tsp dried)

1.2 litres chicken stock

4 medium tomatoes, skinned, deseeded and diced

salt and freshly ground black pepper

a few oregano sprigs, to garnish

1 Soak the beans in separate bowls overnight in plenty of water.
2 Drain and rinse the beans. Place the borlotti beans in a large saucepan, cover with fresh water and bring to the boil. Add the cannellini beans 15 minutes later. Cook for 1 hour, or until soft. Test for doneness, as they may take a little longer. Drain and set aside.
3 Heat some oil in a large saucepan, add the pancetta and sauté on a medium heat for a couple of minutes. Add the carrots, celery and leek and sauté for 5–6 minutes.
4 Stir in the garlic, bay leaves and oregano. Pour in the stock, add the beans and simmer for about 30 minutes, until all the flavours infuse and the beans have softened.
5 Stir in the diced tomatoes and simmer for another 5 minutes. Check for seasoning and serve, garnishing with oregano sprigs.

KEEPING IT LOCAL: TRY ADDING GUBBEEN SMOKED BACON OR EVEN LOCALLY MADE FENNEL AND SAGE SAUSAGES TO THE SOUP, MAKING IT A MEAL IN ONE.

GREEN BEANS WITH SESAME SEEDS

FAGIOLINI CON SEMI DI SESAMO / SERVES 4

A SIMPLE RECIPE FOR FRESH GARDEN GREEN BEANS THAT TAKES NO TIME AT ALL. THE CHILLI FLAKES GIVE IT A LITTLE LIFT!

300g green beans, washed and trimmed
2 tbsp extra virgin olive oil
$1/2$ tsp red chilli flakes
1 garlic clove, thinly sliced
2 tbsp sesame seeds

1 Steam the beans until just tender and set aside.
2 Heat the olive oil in a saucepan over a low heat. Add the red chilli flakes and sauté for 1 minute. Add the sliced garlic and sauté for a further minute. Toss the sesame seeds into the olive oil and cook for 1 minute more, until the seeds are golden.
3 Arrange the beans in a bowl and pour the sesame oil over the beans.

KEEPING IT LOCAL: HOME-GROWN LOCAL SPINACH FROM YOUR MARKET IS A GREAT ALTERNATIVE TO THE GREEN BEANS AND IS A WONDERFUL ACCOMPANIMENT TO ROSEMARY ROAST BEEF.

PESTO GENOVESE

MAKES ABOUT 250G

THE PERFECT PESTO IS MADE IN A PESTLE AND MORTAR. IT'S OKAY TO USE A FOOD PROCESSOR, BUT KEEP IT TO YOURSELF!

75g pine nuts, lightly toasted
2 garlic cloves, sliced
100g basil leaves, washed
150ml extra virgin olive oil
30g freshly grated Pecorino
30g freshly grated Parmesan
salt and freshly ground black pepper

1 Place the pine nuts, garlic and a large pinch of salt in a pestle and mortar and pound to a pulp.
2 Add the basil and some of the oil and pound gently, releasing the oils from the basil but retaining some texture.
3 Add in the remaining oil and pound again, then add in the cheeses and check the consistency – it should be thick and drop off the edge of the spoon. Add more olive oil if required. Season to taste.
4 Spoon the pesto into a jar and pour a thin layer of oil over so that the basil holds its colour. Cover well and store in the fridge for up to 10 days.

 KEEPING IT LOCAL: PICK UP SOME POTATOES AND BEANS FRESH FROM THE MARKET AND MAKE SQUIGGLY PASTA WITH PESTO, POTATOES AND BEANS FOR SUPPER (SEE THE RECIPE ON PAGE 37).

BEANS WITH ITALIAN SAUSAGE

FAGIOLI CON SALSICCE ITALIANE / SERVES 4

TRY THIS ONE FOR A HEARTY FAMILY DISH, THE KIND YOU PUT IN THE CENTRE OF THE TABLE AND EVERYONE DIGS IN. ITS SUCCESS IS THE QUALITY OF THE RAW INGREDIENTS, SO GO FOR THE BEST, MOST FLAVOURSOME SAUSAGES. THIS RECIPE CALLS FOR COOKED BEANS, SO I OFTEN USE CANNED BEANS, WASHED AND DRAINED, FOR A SPEEDY DISH.

3 tbsp extra virgin olive oil, plus extra for drizzling

8 Italian sausages

2 garlic cloves, sliced

1 red chilli, finely chopped

2 tsp chopped rosemary

3 celery stalks, finely sliced

2 carrots, diced

500ml vegetable stock

1 tsp chopped thyme

200g cooked borlotti beans

200g cooked cannellini beans

12 cherry tomatoes, washed

1 Heat the olive oil in a large frying pan over a medium heat. Fry the sausages until they're cooked through, then transfer onto a plate. Slice on the diagonal and set aside.

2 Add the garlic, chilli and rosemary to the pan and sauté for 1 minute.

3 Stir in the celery and carrots and simmer for a further 3 minutes. Add the stock and thyme, cover with a lid and simmer for 10 minutes.

4 Return the sausages to the pan and add the beans. Bring to the boil, then reduce the heat and simmer for a further 12 minutes.

5 Stir in the cherry tomatoes and simmer for 2 minutes. Drizzle with olive oil and serve immediately.

KEEPING IT LOCAL: IF I'M SHORT OF INGREDIENTS IN MY GARDEN, I HEAD INTO AN TAIRSEACH, MY LOCAL ORGANIC FARM SHOP RUN BY THE DOMINICAN NUNS IN WICKLOW TOWN, WHERE I CAN STOCK UP ON ALL THE INGREDIENTS FOR THIS DISH. YOU CAN REPLACE THE BEANS WITH NEW SEASON IRISH POTATOES – JUST LEAVE THE SKINS ON AND QUARTER THEM.

BROAD BEAN HUMMUS

CREMA DI FAVE / MAKES ABOUT 250G

THIS IS SO TASTY AND HEALTHY. I STIR THE LEFTOVERS INTO A PASTA SALAD WITH ROCKET. IT'S IDEAL FOR THOSE MOMENTS WHEN UNEXPECTED VISITORS CALL BY IN THE SUMMER.

250g broad beans
5 tbsp extra virgin olive oil
2 garlic cloves, sliced
1 lemon, zest and juice
1 tbsp chopped parsley
salt and freshly ground black pepper
celery sticks, radishes and breadsticks for dipping

1 Boil the broad beans in rapidly boiling water for about 10 minutes, until tender. Drain and set aside.
2 Heat the olive oil in a small saucepan over a low heat. Add the garlic and simmer for a few minutes, taking care not to let the garlic burn.
3 Place the broad beans in a food processor. Add the garlic, oil, lemon zest and juice and process until fairly smooth. Add the parsley and season to taste.

KEEPING IT LOCAL: NO NEED TO SHOP LOCALLY, AS THE BROAD BEANS GROW SO EASILY IN THE GARDEN – YOU DON'T HAVE TO BE TOO 'GREEN FINGERED', HONESTLY! LOCAL RAPESEED OIL IS DELICIOUS IN HUMMUS. TRY SECOND NATURE RAPESEED OIL FROM KILKENNY.

CREAMY PENNETTE WITH WALNUTS

PENNETTE CREMOSE ALLE NOCI / SERVES 4

THIS IS VERY QUICK AND SO EASY – IT'S A NO-COOK SAUCE. I LOVE ITS SIMPLE FLAVOURS, BUT IT CAN BE DRESSED UP A LITTLE MORE BY ADDING SOME LOVELY SMOKED CHICKEN. I USE WHATEVER NUTS I HAVE IN THE STORE CUPBOARD AND IT HAS ALWAYS BEEN A WINNER.

350g pennette
100g soft goats cheese
5 tbsp mascarpone
120g walnuts, toasted and roughly chopped
pinch of nutmeg
50g rocket, washed and trimmed
4 tbsp freshly grated Parmesan
salt and freshly ground black pepper

1 Cook the pasta according to the instructions on the package. Drain, but retain some of the cooking liquid and return the pennette to the saucepan.
2 Add the soft goats cheese and mascarpone to the pasta and stir, adding a little of the reserved liquid as required.
3 Sprinkle over the walnuts and grate a little nutmeg over the top. Add the rocket and Parmesan and carefully mix. Season to taste and serve immediately.

KEEPING IT LOCAL: I LOVE TO ADD A FEW THINLY SLICED ROASTED BEETROOT SLICES, WHICH ALSO GIVES THIS DISH A PRETTY PINK COLOUR.

GREEN AND WHITE BEAN SALAD

INSALATA DI FAGIOLINI E FAGIOLI / SERVES 4

THERE IS GREAT COLOUR IN THIS SALAD AND IT'S EASY TO ARRANGE FOR A RELAXED LUNCHEON, AS MOST OF THESE INGREDIENTS WOULD BE IN YOUR STORE CUPBOARD OR IN THE VEGETABLE GARDEN.

120g dried cannellini beans, soaked overnight
200g French beans, topped and sliced lengthways
12 black olives, pitted
1 red onion, finely sliced
2 tbsp chopped chives

FOR THE DRESSING:
$1/2$ red chilli, very finely chopped
$1/2$ lemon, zest and juice
6 tbsp extra virgin olive oil
$1/2$ tsp wholegrain honey mustard
salt and freshly ground black pepper

1 To prepare the dressing, whisk together all the ingredients. Season to taste.
2 Drain and rinse the cannellini beans and place in a large saucepan with enough fresh water to cover. Bring to the boil and rapidly cook for 12 minutes, then reduce the heat and simmer for 40–45 minutes, or until tender. Add a little salt during the last 5 minutes of the cooking time.
3 In the meantime, bring a saucepan of water to the boil, add the French beans and cook for 2–3 minutes, until just tender but still crunchy. Drain, then drizzle most of the dressing over the beans while they're still warm.
5 Stir in the olives, onion and chives. Using tongs, arrange the salad on a large platter and spoon over the remaining dressing. Serve immediately.

 KEEPING IT LOCAL: HEAD TO YOUR LOCAL FISHMONGER FOR FRESH PRAWNS. CHARGRILL THEM WITH A DRIZZLE OF LEMON FOR AN EXTRA SPECIAL TREAT TO SERVE WITH THIS VIBRANT SALAD.

GREEN OLIVE AND HAZELNUT PESTO

PESTO ALLE OLIVE VERDI E NOCCIOLE / MAKES ABOUT 350G

WHEN NOT TOSSING IT WITH PASTA, I DRIZZLE THIS OVER STEAMED ASPARAGUS OR USE IT AS A DIP FOR HONEY-ROASTED PARSNIP CRISPS. I THINK IT'S BETTER NOT TO PROCESS IT TOO SMOOTHLY – LEAVE SOME TEXTURE.

200g green olives, pitted and drained
100g hazelnuts, toasted
3 garlic cloves, roughly chopped
zest of 1 lemon and juice of ½
1 tbsp capers, drained
200ml extra virgin olive oil
30g rocket leaves, washed and trimmed
50g freshly grated Parmesan
salt and freshly ground black pepper

1   Place the olives, hazelnuts, garlic, lemon zest and juice and capers into a food processor and pulse a few times, until roughly chopped.
2   While the motor is still running, slowly pour in the olive oil. Add the rocket leaves and pulse until fairly smooth. Add the Parmesan and season to taste.
3   Cover well and store in the fridge for up to 10 days.

KEEPING IT LOCAL: DESMOND CHEESE IS A WONDERFUL ALTERNATIVE TO PARMESAN IN THIS RECIPE.

VEGETABLES
& SALADS

THE CLEVER APPROACH TO INCLUDING AS MANY
VEGETABLES AS POSSIBLE IN YOUR DIET IS TO
INCORPORATE THEM INTO ALMOST EVERY PART OF THE
MEAL, AND THAT IS EXACTLY WHAT THE SAVVY ITALIANS
DO. FOR ANTIPASTI, THERE ARE MARINATED ARTICHOKES
AND PEPPERS, CAPONATA AND THE LIKE. SOUP MIGHT
BE MINESTRONE, WITH PLENTY OF TOMATOES, ONIONS,
CARROTS AND CELERY. THE PASTA COURSE IS LIKELY
TO HAVE A SAUCE MADE FROM VEGETABLES AND
VEGETABLES ACCOMPANY THE MAIN COURSE. EVEN PIZZA
IS TOPPED WITH VEGETABLES!

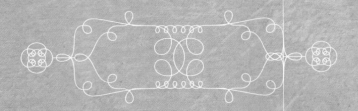

GARLIC

A lovely phrase about cooking garlic that I learned from Claudio's cousin Antonio is that 'when it dances, it's ready'. Simply cover the base of the saucepan with olive oil and when it's nicely warm, add in the sliced garlic. Within about 1 minute, the garlic starts to move, as if it's waltzing – if it starts to do the tango, you're in trouble, as it's heading towards burnt.

Garlic is so easy to grow – just plant the clove when it has sprouted and it grows into a bulb. With a few bulbs in your garden, you can practise your plaiting skills later and store it for the winter.

WILD GARLIC

Wild garlic grows on the forest floor and has a beautiful white flower. There is a broad leaf cousin that grows in the hedges along the roads here and blooms in late spring. In both cases, you will smell it before you see it!

Carefully forage for healthy wild garlic, away from traffic, using a pair of scissors to snip the garlic off. Give it a good wash before using.

TOMATOES

I know that it's officially a fruit, but as it's more savoury, I'm taking the liberty of adding tomatoes to the vegetable section.

At the markets in Italy, it's very common for a stallholder to only sell tomatoes, with all types on offer depending on the cook's needs, from deliciously sweet green tomatoes for salads to plump juicy ones for making sauces. The vendor is always ready to advise and before long, you'll find yourself being talked into cooking a totally different recipe than the one you had originally intended, such is their enthusiasm.

Da salsa is the term used to refer to tomatoes suitable for making classic tomato sauce. The most well-known variety is San Marzano, an heirloom tomato that grows on the sides of Mount Vesuvius. In the Fulvio household, this is our favourite canned tomato. The plum tomato is also used in sauces for its wonderful intense red colour and richness and is slightly sweet. They also dry very well.

On the other side of the tomato balance is the *insalataro* type, which are salad tomatoes. Favourites here are the Tuscan Costoluto and the world-famous little Pachino from Sicily, which is my favourite.

SQUASH

As you travel around Italy there are endless fields of green leaves, and just underneath are these magical gems in all shapes and sizes. Zucchini (courgettes) are well-known, but there's a huge variety at the markets, especially in Sicily. The courgette flowers are delicious dipped in a light batter and fried.

In autumn, Lombardy explodes with winter squash of all varieties, such as Marina di Chioggia, Berettina, Zucca Blu and Zucca Tonda Padana. Among the many uses for squash is to pickle them by adding mustard seeds to form the most delicious *mostarda* (see page 100).

ARTICHOKE, ROAST PARSNIP AND WALNUT SALAD

INSALATA DI CARCIOFI, PASTINACHE ARROSTITE E NOCI / SERVES 4

FOR THE LAST TWO YEARS, ARTICHOKES FLOURISHED IN MY VEGETABLE GARDEN. WE HAD SO MANY, I EVEN USED THE GORGEOUS PURPLE FLOWERS FOR ARRANGEMENTS TO BRING MORE OF THE OUTDOORS INDOORS.

extra virgin olive oil

4–5 parsnips, sliced into thin wedges

rocket or any favourite garden leaves

12 artichoke hearts, cut into wedges

12 cherry tomatoes, washed and halved

100g walnuts, lightly toasted and roughly chopped

rosemary croutons, to garnish (see below)

FOR THE DRESSING:

2 tbsp walnut oil

1 tbsp sunflower oil

1 tbsp white wine vinegar

1 ½ tsp wholegrain mustard

salt and freshly ground black pepper

1 Preheat the oven to 180°C/fan 160°C/gas 4.

2 Combine all the ingredients for the dressing in a jar with a lid and shake to combine. Season to taste.

3 Drizzle a roasting pan with olive oil, toss the parsnips in and roast for about 20 minutes, until crisp and golden.

4 Arrange the rocket or other garden leaves on a serving platter.

5 Mix the artichoke wedges, cherry tomatoes and walnuts with a little dressing in a bowl.

6 Arrange the parsnips around the edge of the leaves. Spoon the artichokes, cherry tomatoes and walnuts onto the rocket.

7 Drizzle with a little more dressing and garnish with rosemary croutons.

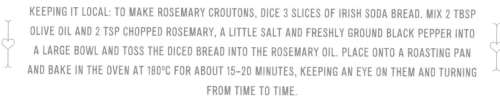

KEEPING IT LOCAL: TO MAKE ROSEMARY CROUTONS, DICE 3 SLICES OF IRISH SODA BREAD. MIX 2 TBSP OLIVE OIL AND 2 TSP CHOPPED ROSEMARY, A LITTLE SALT AND FRESHLY GROUND BLACK PEPPER INTO A LARGE BOWL AND TOSS THE DICED BREAD INTO THE ROSEMARY OIL. PLACE ONTO A ROASTING PAN AND BAKE IN THE OVEN AT 180ºC FOR ABOUT 15–20 MINUTES, KEEPING AN EYE ON THEM AND TURNING FROM TIME TO TIME.

ASPARAGUS WITH PISTACHIO ORANGE DRESSING

ASPARAGI CON SALSA DI PISTACCHIO E ARANCIO / SERVES 4

AS MUCH AS I LOVE ASPARAGUS, THE DRESSING IN THIS RECIPE IS AMAZING AND FOR ONCE, ASPARAGUS TAKES A BACK SEAT. I REALLY LOOK FORWARD TO THE ASPARAGUS SEASON SO THAT WE CAN SERVE THIS DRESSING.

20 asparagus spears, woody ends removed
50g butter
3 tbsp pistachio nuts
1 orange, zest and juice
1 tsp chopped dill
salt and freshly ground black pepper
a few dill sprigs, to garnish

1   Steam the asparagus until it's just tender and set aside.
2   In the meantime, melt the butter in a small frying pan over a low heat. Add the pistachios and toast the nuts until they're lightly browned. Stir in the orange zest, juice and dill. Season to taste.
3   Arrange the asparagus on a serving platter. Spoon the dressing over the warm asparagus, garnish with sprigs of dill and serve immediately.

KEEPING IT LOCAL: TRY THIS DRESSING WITH CURLY KALE IN THE WINTER. WE HAVE PURPLE CURLY KALE IN THE GARDEN – IT LOOKS AND TASTES GREAT.

BUTTERNUT SQUASH, RED ONION AND SPINACH SALAD WITH A SESAME DRESSING

INSALATA DI ZUCCA, CIPOLLE ROSSE E SPINACI CON UNA SALSA DI SESAMO / SERVES 4

THIS SESAME DRESSING MAY NOT BE TRADITIONALLY ITALIAN, BUT IT'S DELICIOUS. CHARGRILL THE BUTTERNUT SQUASH SO THAT THE NATURAL SUGARS CARAMELISE TO BRING A LOVELY SWEETNESS TO THIS SALAD.

1 butternut squash, peeled and sliced into wedges

2 red onions, peeled and cut into wedges

1 tbsp extra virgin olive oil

salt and freshly ground black pepper

100g baby spinach leaves, watercress or your favourite salad leaves, trimmed and washed

12-14 seedless red grapes, halved

100g walnuts

Parmesan shavings

FOR THE DRESSING:

3 tbsp sesame seeds, toasted

3 tbsp extra virgin olive oil

1 tbsp white wine vinegar

$^{1}/_{2}$ tsp Dijon mustard

salt and freshly ground pepper

1 Preheat the oven to 180°C/fan 160°C/gas 4.

2 Combine all the ingredients for the dressing in a bottle with a lid and shake to combine.

3 Brush the butternut wedges and onion with oil and some salt and pepper and roast for 20–25 minutes, until soft.

4 In the meantime, combine the spinach and grapes with some of the dressing and place on a large serving platter.

5 Add the warm butternut squash wedges and onions, sprinkle over the walnuts and the Parmesan shavings and drizzle a little more dressing over. Serve immediately.

 KEEPING IT LOCAL: USE WEDGES OF PARSNIPS TO REPLACE THE BUTTERNUT SQUASH AND TRY USING DERRYCAMMA FARM RAPESEED OIL FOR A WONDERFUL HEALTHY OPTION.

FENNEL PURÉE

PUREA DI FINOCCHIO / SERVES 4

A STAPLE FOOD IN ITALY, ESPECIALLY IN THE SOUTH, IT'S SURPRISING HOW EASILY FENNEL GROWS HERE IN IRELAND. BY ADDING A FEW FENNEL SEEDS TO THIS RECIPE, IT GIVES THE ANISE FLAVOUR A LIFT.

2 tbsp extra virgin olive oil
2 large fennel bulbs, roughly chopped
100ml cream
100ml chicken stock
$1/2$ lemon, zest only
salt and freshly ground black pepper

1 Heat the olive oil in a large saucepan, add the fennel and cover with a lid. Cook on a low heat until the fennel is tender.
2 Place the cooked fennel in a food processor and add the cream, stock and lemon zest. Blend until smooth.
3 Season to taste, then return the fennel purée to a saucepan and gently reheat before serving.

KEEPING IT LOCAL: DEPENDING ON AVAILABILITY,
I REPLACE THE FENNEL WITH THE HUMBLE CAULIFLOWER.

CHARGRILLED SUMMER VEGETABLES WITH CHILLI BASIL DRESSING

VERDURE GRIGLIATE CON SALSA PICCANTE E BASILICO / SERVES 4–6

IT ISN'T A TYPING ERROR IN THE RECIPE BELOW, THERE REALLY IS WHITE WINE IN THE DRESSING. YUM!

8–12 cherry tomatoes

6 small shallots, peeled and halved

2 courgettes, chopped into wedges

2 aubergines, sliced

1 red pepper, sliced

1 yellow pepper, sliced

3 rosemary sprigs

salt and freshly ground black pepper

FOR THE DRESSING:

150ml extra virgin olive oil

100ml white wine

12 basil leaves, torn, plus whole leaves to garnish

2 garlic cloves, finely sliced

½ red chilli, finely chopped

salt and freshly ground black pepper

1 Combine all the ingredients for the dressing in a jar with a lid and shake to combine.

2 Place all the vegetables and the rosemary sprigs in a roasting pan. Pour over most of the dressing, retaining one-third for later, and allow to marinate for 1 hour, turning the vegetables occasionally.

3 Preheat the BBQ to a medium heat.

4 Drain the vegetables, place on the BBQ and chargrill on both sides, turning from time to time and brushing with the marinade.

5 When cooked through, season to taste, then place on a serving platter and drizzle with the remaining dressing. Garnish with the whole basil leaves.

KEEPING IT LOCAL: I HAVE ALSO SERVED THIS AS PART OF AN ANTIPASTO PLATTER WITH JACK MCCARTHY'S SLIABH LUACHRA AIR-DRIED BEEF AND LOTS OF CRUSTY BREAD.

FIELD MUSHROOMS STUFFED WITH BACON AND SPINACH

FUNGHI RIPIENI DI PANCETTA E SPINACI / SERVES 4

FOR A LIGHT LUNCH I SIMPLY REPLACE THE BACON WITH SOME CRUMBLED GOATS CHEESE. THIS IS ALSO A NICE STARTER FOR A DINNER PARTY.

4 field mushrooms, wiped clean and stalks removed and chopped

1 tbsp extra virgin olive oil

75g bacon lardons

60g baby spinach leaves, washed and chopped

2 garlic cloves, thinly sliced

4 tbsp breadcrumbs

4 basil leaves, shredded

1 tbsp chopped parsley

salt and freshly ground black pepper

crostini, to serve

green salad, to serve

1　Preheat the oven to 200°C/fan 180°C/gas 6.

2　Arrange the mushroom caps on an oiled baking tray.

3　Heat the olive oil in a frying pan over a medium heat. Add the bacon and fry until crisp and golden. Add the chopped mushroom stalks to the bacon and cook for 1 minute. Stir in the spinach and sliced garlic and sauté for 1–2 minutes. Add the breadcrumbs, basil and parsley. Season to taste.

4　Spoon the bacon and spinach stuffing into the mushrooms. Bake in the preheated oven for 8–10 minutes, until crisp and golden. Serve immediately on crostini with a green salad.

KEEPING IT LOCAL: YOU CAN'T GET MORE LOCAL THAN MUSHROOMS, BACON AND SPINACH, BUT HOW ABOUT USING THE STUFFING IN THIS RECIPE AS A TOPPING ON A LOVELY BAKED POTATO FOR SUPPER?

PUMPKIN *MOSTARDA*

MOSTARDA DI ZUCCA / MAKES 500G

THIS IS A SLIGHTLY DIFFERENT OPTION TO THIS NORTHERN ITALIAN CLASSIC WITH A MUSTARD KICK, WHICH IS SERVED WITH RICH CHEESE AND MEATS. *MOSTARDA DI CREMONA* IS THE MORE TRADITIONAL RECIPE USING FRUITS RANGING FROM FIGS AND PEARS TO QUINCE. THIS CONDIMENT IS DELICIOUS WITH CHEESE AND MEATS.

300g sugar
280ml water
50ml dry white wine
1 lemon, zest and juice
3 tbsp dry mustard
400g pumpkin, sliced into small wedges

1 Line a baking tray with parchment paper.
2 Place the sugar, water, wine, lemon zest and juice and dry mustard into a large saucepan and whisk while bringing it to the boil. Allow to simmer for about 6 minutes to form a thick syrup.
3 Add the pumpkin wedges and poach for about 15 minutes, until nicely tender. Using a slotted spoon, transfer the pumpkin onto the lined baking tray to cool. Retain the syrup.
4 Once the pumpkin has cooled, place it in a jar and pour over the syrup. The slices will keep for a few weeks in the fridge.

  KEEPING IT LOCAL: WE'RE QUITE LUCKY TO BE CLOSE TO SWEETBANK FARM, WHO HAVE THE MOST BEAUTIFUL SUMMER AND AUTUMNAL FRUITS, INCLUDING PEARS. CHOOSE SOME LOCAL CONCORDE OR CONFERENCE PEAR VARIETIES, AS THEY HAVE A LOVELY LONG ELONGATED SHAPE WHICH, WHEN SLICED INTO WEDGES, LOOKS VERY ATTRACTIVE SERVED ON A CHEESE BOARD.

PARMESAN MASHED POTATOES

PUREA AL PARMIGIANO / SERVES 4

THIS IS MY VERSION OF ITALIAN CHAMP – WELL, ALMOST! I CUT BACK ON THE AMOUNT OF SALT TO SEASON HERE BECAUSE THE PARMESAN HAS SO MUCH FLAVOUR.

800g good mashing potatoes, such as Roosters, Maris Piper or Orla, peeled and cut into chunks
4 thyme sprigs
180ml milk
80ml cream
30g butter
salt and freshly ground black pepper
5 spring onions, finely sliced
5 tbsp freshly grated Parmesan

1 Steam the potatoes and thyme together until soft. Remove the thyme sprigs, and while the potatoes are still warm, press them through a potato ricer into a large bowl.
2 In the meantime, add the milk, cream, butter and some salt and pepper to a saucepan and warm through until the butter melts.
3 Pour the milk mixture into the riced potatoes and add the spring onions and Parmesan. Check for seasoning and serve.

KEEPING IT LOCAL: ROOSTERS ARE ALWAYS RELIABLE FOR PERFECT MASH, BUT IN THE SUMMER I LIKE TO USE ORLA POTATOES FROM OUR COOKERY SCHOOL GARDEN.

POOR PEOPLE'S POTATOES

PATATE DEI POVERI / SERVES 4

ORIGINALLY A STAPLE DURING LEANER TIMES, THERE ARE MANY VERSIONS OF THIS RECIPE. TO LIGHTEN THE RECIPE, I'VE REDUCED THE AMOUNT OF OLIVE OIL IN IT SO IT WON'T BE THE TRADITIONAL ONE THAT YOU MAY KNOW, BUT IT'S STILL DELICIOUS.

150ml extra virgin olive oil
800g potatoes, peeled and sliced
3 garlic cloves, left whole
1 ¹/₂ tsp chopped thyme
salt and freshly ground black pepper
2 tbsp chopped parsley

1 Preheat the oven to 200°C/fan 180°C/gas 6.
2 Pour the olive oil into a roasting pan and heat in the oven. Carefully take the pan out of the oven, add the potatoes and sprinkle over the garlic and thyme. Using a fish slice, turn over the potatoes and return the pan to the oven.
3 Roast for 20 minutes, turning from time to time, until the potatoes are crisp and golden. Season to taste.
4 Sprinkle over the parsley and serve immediately.

KEEPING IT LOCAL: USE FINELY SLICED PARSNIPS, LEEKS AND ROSEMARY FOR A CHANGE.

PURPLE SPROUTING BROCCOLI WITH WATERCRESS MAYONNAISE

BROCCOLETTI CON MAIONESE AL CRESCIONE / SERVES 4

THIS IS SO VERSATILE, ANY GARDEN GREENS WILL BE DELICIOUS IN THIS RECIPE. RAINBOW CHARD IS PARTICULARLY GOOD WITH THIS ZINGY DRESSING.

16 stems of purple sprouting broccoli, washed

FOR THE WATERCRESS MAYONNAISE:
2 egg yolks
2 tbsp lemon juice
1 tbsp tarragon vinegar
1 tsp Dijon mustard
$^{1}/_{2}$ tsp paprika
200ml extra virgin olive oil
100g watercress, finely chopped
salt and freshly ground black pepper

1 To make the mayonnaise, whisk together the egg yolks, lemon juice, vinegar, mustard and paprika in a bowl or combine in your food processor. Slowly pour the olive oil in while still whisking. The mixture will emulsify to form a mayonnaise. Stir in the watercress, season to taste and set aside.
2 Steam the purple sprouting broccoli in a steamer until it's just tender. Remove from the steamer and place on a serving platter.
3 Drizzle the mayonnaise over the warm broccoli and serve immediately.

KEEPING IT LOCAL: SERVE THIS MAYONNAISE WITH LOCALLY CAUGHT FISH, SUCH AS AVONMORE RIVER TROUT, INSTEAD OF THE BROCCOLI.

TOMATO FENNEL SOUP

ZUPPA DI POMODORO E FINOCCHIO / SERVES 4

HAVING THE CHOPPED FENNEL IN THIS SOUP MEANS THERE IS NO NEED FOR EXTRA HERBS OR ANYTHING ELSE. THIS IS A LOVELY CLASSIC SOUTHERN ITALIAN COMBINATION AND THE BEAUTY OF THE DISH IS ITS SIMPLE, EARTHY FLAVOURS.

2 tbsp extra virgin olive oil
2 fennel bulbs, diced
1 red pepper, diced
2 garlic cloves, thinly sliced
400g tinned chopped tomatoes
800ml chicken stock
2 tbsp tomato purée
salt and freshly ground black pepper

1 Heat the olive oil in a large saucepan. Add the fennel and red pepper and sauté on a low heat until softened. Add the garlic and cook for 1 minute more.
2 Add the tomatoes, stock and tomato purée and simmer for 20–25 minutes.
3 Pour into a food processer and blend until smooth. Return to the pan and heat through. Season to taste and serve.

KEEPING IT LOCAL: IN THE SUMMER, WE MAKE COURGETTE AND FENNEL SOUP HERE AT BALLYKNOCKEN, AS WE SEEM TO HAVE AN ENDLESS SUPPLY OF COURGETTES. I THINK IT HAS SOMETHING TO DO WITH THE AMPLE QUANTITIES OF RAIN MIXED WITH THE SUNSHINE!

WILD GARLIC AND ROCKET SOUP

ZUPPA DI AGLIO SELVATICO E RUCOLA / SERVES 4

THE WILD GARLIC GIVES THIS SOUP A BEAUTIFUL PALE GREEN COLOUR AND IS CONTRASTED BY THE DARKER GREEN ROCKET.

2 tbsp extra virgin olive oil
1 leek, finely chopped
4 potatoes, peeled and diced
1 large bunch wild garlic, washed and roughly chopped
1.5 litres vegetable stock
1 tsp chopped thyme
salt and freshly ground black pepper
50g rocket, rinsed and roughly chopped

1 Heat the olive oil in a large saucepan. Add the leek and sauté for about 4 minutes. Add the potatoes, cover and sauté until softened but not brown, stirring from time to time. You may like to add a little stock at this stage to prevent the potatoes from sticking to the bottom of the pot.

2 Add the wild garlic, stock and thyme. Bring to the boil and simmer for about 3 minutes.

3 Pour the soup into a blender and process until smooth. Season to taste. Return the soup to the pot, stir through the rocket and serve immediately.

KEEPING IT LOCAL: WHEN WILD GARLIC IS OUT OF SEASON, DRIZZLE 1 LARGE WHOLE, UNPEELED GARLIC BULB WITH OLIVE OIL AND ROAST FOR ABOUT 20 MINUTES AT 180°C.

WARM RADICCHIO, SPINACH AND BASIL SALAD

INSALATA DI RADICCHIO CALDI, SPINACI E BASILICO / SERVES 4

MOVE OVER, POPEYE! THIS IS THE DISH TO IMPROVE YOUR VITAMIN C AND IRON LEVELS AND IT'S VERY TASTY TOO.

200g baby spinach leaves, washed and trimmed

10 basil leaves, washed

2 radicchio, washed and sliced into wedges

1 tbsp extra virgin oil

Parmesan shavings, to garnish

5 tbsp pine nuts, toasted, to garnish

FOR THE DRESSING:

100ml extra virgin olive oil

2 garlic cloves, thinly sliced

½ red chilli, finely chopped

2 tbsp chopped chives

salt and freshly ground black pepper

1 Arrange the spinach and basil leaves in a large salad bowl.
2 Heat a medium-sized grill pan over a medium heat. Brush the radicchio generously with the olive oil and chargrill it lightly, then add to the salad bowl.
3 In the meantime, to make the dressing, heat the olive oil in a saucepan. Add the garlic and chilli and simmer for a few minutes, stirring from time to time. Cool slightly, then add the chives and season to taste.
4 Spoon the warm dressing over the spinach, basil and radicchio. Scatter the Parmesan shavings and pine nuts on top and serve immediately.

 KEEPING IT LOCAL: TRY THIS WITH MOONSHINE FARM'S UNA CHEESE, A LOVELY SOFT CHEESE WITH SUNDRIED TOMATOES. YOU CAN EVEN ADD SOME PLUMS FOR SWEETNESS – SIMPLY POACH PLUM WEDGES IN A LITTLE RED WINE, CINNAMON AND SUGAR AND ADD TO THE SALAD.

ZUCCHINI STUFFED WITH RAGÙ

ZUCCHINE RIPIENE AL RAGÙ / SERVES 4

I HAD THE PLEASURE OF ENJOYING THIS DISH IN THE CASTLE OF THE BORGHESE FAMILY JUST OUTSIDE OF ROME. THE WONDERFUL COMPANY OF THESE INTRIGUING ARISTOCRATS COUPLED WITH THEIR DELICIOUS HOME COOKING WAS A MOMENT IN MY LIFE THAT I WON'T EVER FORGET.

2 large courgettes
3 tbsp breadcrumbs
2 tbsp freshly grated Parmesan
1 tbsp chopped parsley

FOR THE RAGÙ:
extra virgin olive oil
100g pancetta
500g minced beef
2 carrots, finely diced
1 onion, finely chopped
1 celery stalk, finely sliced
1 garlic clove, finely chopped
400ml vegetable stock
100ml red wine
1 tsp tomato purée
salt and freshly ground black pepper

FOR THE TOMATO SAUCE:
2 tbsp extra virgin olive oil
2 garlic cloves, finely chopped
1 tsp tomato purée
400g tinned whole plum tomatoes, crushed
salt and freshly ground black pepper
sugar
5 large basil leaves, shredded

1 Preheat the oven to 180°C/fan 160°C/gas 4.
2 Cut the courgettes into 4cm lengths and scoop out the centre. Chop the scooped-out flesh for the ragu.
3 To make the ragù, heat a large saucepan with a little oil and add the pancetta. Fry until it's crisp and brown. Remove some of the oil, add the minced beef and sauté until brown. Stir in the carrots, onion, celery and chopped courgette. Cook for about 5 minutes before adding the garlic, vegetable stock, wine, tomato purée and salt and freshly ground black pepper. Allow to simmer for 30–35 minutes, until a thick ragu has formed.
4 To make the tomato sauce, heat the olive oil in a large pan. Add the garlic and cook for about 2 minutes on a low heat, until soft. Add the tomato purée and cook for a further 1 minute. Add the tomatoes with their juices and season with salt and pepper. Bring to the boil, reduce the heat and simmer for about 20 minutes, until the sauce has thickened. Check the seasoning and add a little sugar if necessary. When you're about to serve, add some shredded basil leaves to the sauce.

5 Combine the breadcrumbs, Parmesan and parsley in a bowl.

6 Spoon the ragu into the courgette slices, sprinkle over the breadcrumb mix and place the filled courgettes on an oiled baking tray. Bake for 25–30 minutes, until the courgette softens and the breadcrumbs are golden.

7 To serve, spoon some of the tomato sauce onto a warm serving bowl or platter and place the courgettes on top of the sauce. Serve immediately.

KEEPING IT LOCAL: ASK YOUR LOCAL BUTCHER FOR SMOKED BACON AND MINCED PORK INSTEAD OF THE PANCETTA AND BEEF. FERMANAGH OAK SMOKED BLACK BACON WOULD BE A LOVELY ALTERNATIVE TO THE PANCETTA.

OLIVES & OLIVE OIL

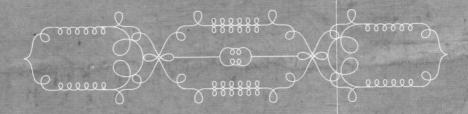

THERE ARE DOZENS OF OLIVE VARIETIES THROUGHOUT ITALY, SO OLIVE OIL AND TABLE OLIVES ARE VERY REGIONAL AND DISTINCTIVE BY COLOUR AND FLAVOUR. FOR EXAMPLE, IN SICILY THE WONDERFUL CASTELVETRANO OLIVE – ALSO KNOWN AS NOCELLARA DEL BELICE – PRODUCES AN EARTHY, BUTTERY OLIVE OIL, WHILE THE TAGGIASCA FROM LIGURIA, A SOFT BROWN OLIVE, PRODUCES A LIGHT, ROUNDED FLAVOUR. AS TABLE OLIVES, THE TAGGIASCA ARE PICKED WHEN BLACK, THEN BRINED, SO THEY HAVE A DISTINCTIVE BROWNISH COLOUR. IN MY OPINION, THEY ARE A DELICACY.

THE BUSINESS OF OLIVE OIL IS VITAL TO THE REGIONS AND MANY HAVE ACHIEVED DOP STATUS (*DENOMINAZIONE D'ORIGINE PROTETTA*, OR PROTECTED DESIGNATION OF ORIGIN), WHICH SETS OUT CLEAR REGULATIONS REGARDING THE PRODUCTION FROM START TO FINISH AND THEREBY PROTECTS THE STANDARDS AND UNIQUENESS OF EACH REGION.

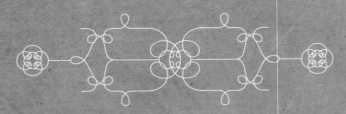

At the olive groves of Frantoi Cutrera in Sicily, the owner told me the story of when tractors were introduced in the 1950s to pick the olives. Prior to that, all olives had been painstakingly picked by hand. The olive trees didn't produce any fruit for two whole years and the locals said it was because the trees were upset that machines were now doing the job. (A good explanation would be that the tractor vibrations upset the roots of the trees, but I prefer the other story.)

I happen to possess the world's most expensive olive oil. I had the pleasure of meeting the delightful movie director and olive farmer Armando Manni, who produces an exceptional organic olive oil from his farm in the Tuscan hills. He regaled me with stories of how celebrities rub this oil into their skin. He very generously gifted me a bottle of this oil. I was thrilled. I suddenly had a taste of this celebrity extravagance. But this gift has caused me a dilemma. What is a food lover and cook like me to do with a bottle of the world's most expensive oil? It sat in a dark cupboard, untouched. Yes, I too could rub it on my skin, but surely that would leave me without having really experienced this golden nectar. There was only one answer – I would rub it onto salad leaves and enjoy it for its first purpose in life.

HOW TO USE OLIVE OIL

As a guideline, finish a dish with the best oil. The most expensive, extra virgin, is for salads and drizzling. The rule used to be that other olive oils were acceptable for frying and cooking. That said, there are so many extra virgin olive oils available today at reasonable prices that they are my preferred choice to cook with.

Store olive oil in a cool place in a dark glass bottle.

CITRUS-MARINATED OLIVES

OLIVE MARINATE AGLI AGRUMI / MAKES 500G

THESE ARE GREAT FOR COCKTAIL PARTIES AND TO SERVE FOR NIBBLES WHEN THE FAMILY COME AROUND FOR AN EVENING GATHERING. EASY TO PREPARE, THEY CAN BE MADE WELL IN ADVANCE.

200g black olives

200g green olives

250ml extra virgin olive oil, sufficient to ensure olives are covered in the saucepan

4 garlic cloves, finely sliced

1 red chilli, finely chopped

1 orange, zest and juice

1/2 lemon, zest and juice

2 tbsp chopped parsley

1 Place all the ingredients in a large saucepan. Bring to the boil then simmer for 2 minutes, then remove from the heat.

2 Allow to cool, then spoon into a sterilised jar. These will keep for 2 weeks in the fridge.

KEEPING IT LOCAL: ADD CUBED ST TOLA'S GREEK-STYLE CHEESE TO THE OLIVES AND MARINATE FOR A FEW DAYS.

CHILLI OLIVE OIL

OLIO D'OLIVA AL PEPERONCINO / MAKES ABOUT 500ML

FLAVOURED OLIVE OILS ARE A GREAT FAVOURITE OF MINE. THERE ARE SO MANY COMBINATIONS: BASIL AND THYME OR GARLIC, PEPPERCORN AND LAVENDER AND OF COURSE THE LEMON OIL I USE SO OFTEN WHEN ROASTING MY VEGETABLES.

500ml extra virgin olive oil   5–6 red chillies   1 tbsp green peppercorns

1 Pour the olive oil into a saucepan, then add the chillies and peppercorns. Heat the oil to 180°C.
2 Allow to cool, then using a funnel, carefully pour into sterilised bottles and secure with a lid. Store in a cool, dark place for 2 weeks before using.

KEEPING IT LOCAL: DURING THE SUMMER, I OFTEN HAVE A GREAT CROP OF RED CHILLIES FROM MY GREENHOUSE. I DRY SOME OF THEM AND USE OTHERS FOR THIS FLAVOURED OLIVE OIL.

ROSEMARY AND GARLIC OLIVE OIL

OLIO D'OLIVA AL ROSMARINO ED AGLIO / MAKES ABOUT 500ML

500ml extra virgin olive oil   5–6 garlic cloves, peeled   4 rosemary sprigs, washed and patted dry

1 Pour the olive oil into a saucepan, then add the garlic and rosemary sprigs. Heat the oil to 180°C.
2 Allow to cool, then using a funnel, carefully pour into sterilised bottles and secure with a lid. Store in a cool, dark place for 2 weeks before using.

KEEPING IT LOCAL: USE DONEGAL RAPESEED OIL INSTEAD OF OLIVE OIL AND YOUR GARDEN ROSEMARY OR THYME, WHICH ARE EASY TO CULTIVATE.

OLIVE OIL ICE CREAM

GELATO ALL'OLIO D'OLIVA / MAKES 750ML

WHO CAN RESIST A GOOD HOMEMADE ICE CREAM AS A TREAT? THIS ICE CREAM MIGHT SOUND BIZARRE, BUT TAKE IT FROM ME, IT'S ABSOLUTELY DELICIOUS! SERVE WITH BISCOTTI OR THIN, CRISPY CHOCOLATE CHIP BISCUITS AND A CARAMEL BALSAMIC DRIZZLE.

300ml milk
250ml double cream
100g caster sugar
6 egg yolks
125ml fruity extra virgin olive oil

1 Heat the milk, cream and sugar in a saucepan over a medium heat, stirring until the sugar has dissolved.
2 Place the egg yolks into a bowl and slowly pour in the warm milk mixture, whisking all the time until a thick custard forms.
3 Whisk in the olive oil and pour into an ice cream maker or into a container suitable for the freezer. Freeze for 4 hours, or until crystals form. Using a fork or a beater, roughly break up the crystals and refreeze (or pulse in a food processor). Repeat twice, refreezing for 3–4 hours after each time.

KEEPING IT LOCAL: ADD 4 TBSP SUGAR TO 100ML OF DAVID LLEWELLYN'S BALSAMIC CIDER VINEGAR, REDUCE BY A THIRD, AND YOU WILL HAVE A WONDERFUL SYRUP TO POUR OVER THE ICE CREAM.

CHEESE,
YOGHURT & EGGS

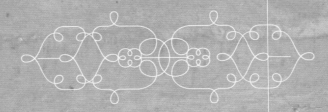

FRESH FARM EGGS, LOCALLY MADE YOGHURTS AND REGIONAL CHEESES ARE ALL INGREDIENTS THAT WE'RE FAMILIAR WITH ON OUR SHORES.

I RECALL MY MOTHER'S INVESTMENT IN A CONTRAPTION CALLED A YOGAMATIC, WHEREBY SHE MADE YOGHURT FROM OUR FRESH UNPASTEURISED FARM MILK. PRIOR TO THAT, WE'D HAD AMPLE EXPERIENCE WITH SUPERMARKET YOGHURT AND LOVED IT, SO YOU CAN IMAGINE OUR SHOCK AT THE FIRST TASTE OF THE HIGHLY ACIDIC HOMEMADE NATURAL YOGHURT. I CAN ONLY DESCRIBE IT AS A JAW-CRUMBLING EXPERIENCE. IT DIDN'T TAKE LONG FOR US TO ADD FARM HONEY OR TABLESPOONS OF HOMEMADE BLACKBERRY JAM TO THE YOGHURT TO REACH THE DESIRED LEVELS OF SWEETNESS. BEFORE LONG, THAT WAS THE ONLY YOGHURT WE WANTED, IT WAS SO CREAMY AND DISTINCTIVE.

CHEESES

We all know the main Italian cheeses – the Pecorino, Mozzarella di Bufala, Gorgonzola and Parmigiano-Reggiano; we might even know Provolone, Taleggio, Asiago and Fontina – but until I met Claudio all those years ago and travelled to the south of Italy, I had never heard of Caciocavallo. Little did I know that in Italy, it holds its own alongside Parmigiano-Reggiano and Pecorino as a leading regional cheese with DOP status. And then there are the soft cheeses such as ricotta and mascarpone. In fact, there are over 450 types of cheese in Italy.

Passion wins over production in cheese-making, where stories abound about the mozzarella makers, especially the plait makers. They say you can tell the humour of the man who made the plait by the cheese. If it's taut or pulled, resulting in a stringiness, he may have been stressed or had a row with his wife that morning. I'm not kidding – just ask in the beguiling Gastronomia Volpetti in Rome. Here are some of my favourites.

- ASIAGO – Made in the Asiago plateau in Veneto, there are two types of this cheese. The softer version is aged for only a few months, while the stronger, nuttier version is aged for up to two and a half years.

- CACIOCAVALLO – Distinctive because of its shape, the name means 'on horseback', as the cheese is paired with its twin and strung over a pole, then left hanging for up to two years to mature. This cheese is native to southern Italy.

- FONTINA – This creamy, buttery cheese is made in the Alpine region on the Swiss border.

- GORGONZOLA – A blue-veined cheese from the outskirts of Milan, the younger version is quite creamy and light. Left to mature, it is nicely crumbly and has a distinct sharpness.

- MOZZARELLA DI BUFALA – Made from the milk of the water buffalo, mozzarella should 'cry tears' when lightly squeezed. In other words, the juices should gently flow. The roots of this cheese date back to the 12th century and is native to the region of Campania.

- PARMIGIANO-REGGIANO – From Lombardy and Emilia-Romagna, this is the king of cheeses. It has the capacity to bring food to life – just a little grating on top of a pasta dish and the dish is transformed from average to exceptional.

- PECORINO – A sheep's cheese with roots in Sardinia, referred to as Pecorino Sardo, it is also made in Tuscany and Sicily, where a delicacy is a version made with locally cultivated saffron. Pecorino Romano is a harder, saltier cheese that is often used to complete pasta dishes such as *Bucatini all'Amatriciana* (see page 12).

- TALEGGIO – Traceable back to the 10th century, this cheese is a soft cheese that is only aged for up to 50 days and is distinctive by its pungent aroma and nutty flavour.

BLACKBERRY AND RASPBERRY YOGHURT ICE CREAM

GELATO ALLO YOGURT DI MORE E LAMPONI / SERVES 4-6

YOGHURT ICE CREAM IS INCREDIBLY POPULAR IN EVERY LOCAL *GELATERIA*. I REALLY LIKE THE BLEND OF TARTNESS FROM THE YOGHURT AND SWEETNESS FROM THE FRUIT, AND IT'S PRETTY HEALTHY TOO. TRY POMEGRANATE IN THIS RECIPE - IT'S A GREAT MEDITERRANEAN FLAVOUR THAT BLENDS WELL WITH THE NATURAL YOGHURT.

200g blackberries, washed
200g raspberries, washed
600ml good-quality natural yoghurt
150ml honey

1 Purée all the ingredients together in a food processor or with a hand blender. Place in an ice cream machine and freeze as per the manufacturer's instructions. Alternatively, if you don't have an ice cream machine, place the mixture in a large plastic container in the freezer. Remove it from the freezer every half hour and give it a thorough mix in a food processor or by hand and refreeze. Repeat this about four times, or until the ice cream is frozen and smooth.

KEEPING IT LOCAL: BLEND SWEETENED POACHED PEACH PURÉE WITH ARDSALLAGH GOATS YOGHURT TO MAKE A LOVELY, DELICIOUS MARBLED YOGHURT ICE CREAM.

WATERCRESS AND HAZELNUT CRUMBED GOATS CHEESE SALAD

INSALATA DI CRESCIONE, NOCCIOLE E FORMAGGIO DI CAPRA / SERVES 4

I HAD A DISH LIKE THIS AROUND THE CORNER FROM THE TREVI FOUNTAIN. WHAT MEMORIES – THAT SALAD HAD GRAPES IN IT, WHICH WAS DELICIOUS TOO.

120g lean smoked bacon, diced

5 tbsp polenta

2 tbsp chopped hazelnuts

4 tbsp seasoned flour

1 egg, beaten

180g goats cheese, sliced

150g watercress, washed and trimmed

FOR THE DRESSING:

120ml extra virgin olive oil

2 tbsp white wine vinegar

2 tsp Dijon mustard

salt and freshly ground black pepper

1 Preheat the oven to 190°C/fan 170°C/gas 5. Lightly oil a shallow ovenproof dish.

2 Place the diced bacon in the dish and cook in the oven until golden, stirring occasionally. Remove from the dish and set aside.

3 Mix the polenta and hazelnuts together and place in a shallow bowl. Place the seasoned flour and the beaten egg in separate shallow bowls.

4 Roll the slices of goats cheese in the flour before dipping into the egg, then roll in the polenta and hazelnuts. Place in the oiled ovenproof dish and bake in the oven for 6–8 minutes, until golden in colour.

5 To make the salad dressing, combine all the ingredients in a jar with a lid and shake vigorously.

6 Toss the watercress in a little dressing and pile onto serving plates. Place the warm goats cheese slices on top. Sprinkle over the crispy bacon and finish with another drizzle of the dressing.

KEEPING IT LOCAL: WATERCRESS GROWS WILD NEAR STREAMS IN THE SPRING. JUST WASH IT VERY WELL BEFORE YOU USE IT.

EGGS *SOFFRITTO*

UOVA AL FORNO CON VERDURE / SERVES 4

SOFFRITTO IS OFTEN CALLED THE HOLY TRINITY OF ANY GOOD SAUCE. IT IS THE BASE INGREDIENTS THAT ARE FRIED INITIALLY AND ARE USUALLY ONIONS, CELERY AND CARROTS AND MAY INCLUDE FLAT-LEAF PARSLEY. BUT IT CAN ALSO BE ANY COMBINATION OF SAUTÉED DELICIOUSNESS THAT FORMS THE FLAVOUR OF A DISH.

extra virgin olive oil

1 onion, chopped

1 red pepper, finely diced

1 tsp chopped rosemary

2 tomatoes, deseeded and diced

2 tbsp freshly grated Parmesan

freshly ground black pepper

4 eggs

4 tbsp breadcrumbs

green salad, to serve

1 Preheat the oven to 180°C/fan 160°C/gas 4. Brush 4 ramekins with olive oil.
2 Heat some olive oil in a saucepan over a low heat and sauté the onion, red pepper and rosemary for about 7 minutes, until soft. Add the tomatoes and cook for 2 minutes.
3 Place 2 tbsp of this cooked *soffritto* into each ramekin. Add some Parmesan and sprinkle with a little black pepper.
4 Crack an egg into each ramekin, sprinkle with breadcrumbs and bake for about 8 minutes, or until the egg is cooked. Serve with a green salad.

KEEPING IT LOCAL: LOCAL FARM EGGS AND SOME DUNLAVIN BACON ARE DELICIOUS IN THE DISH AND MAKE IT A ONE-POT BREAKFAST!

POACHED APPLES STUFFED WITH GORGONZOLA

MELE IN CAMICIA RIPIENE DI GORGONZOLA / SERVES 4–6

WE AUTOMATICALLY THINK OF POACHED PEARS WITH CHEESE, BUT APPLES ARE A LITTLE MORE UNUSUAL AND BRING A WHOLE NEW TWIST TO A TRADITIONAL COMBINATION. KEEP THE LEFTOVER POACHING LIQUID FOR DRIZZLING OVER DESSERTS AND ICE CREAM.

300ml red wine

200ml water

100ml Marsala

50g caster sugar

4 tbsp honey

1 lemon, zest and juice

2 rosemary sprigs

6 Golden Delicious apples, halved and cored

garden salad leaves

160g Gorgonzola, crumbled

3 tbsp roughly chopped walnuts

1 Combine the red wine, water, Marsala, sugar, honey, lemon zest and juice and rosemary in a saucepan. Bring to the boil and simmer for 5 minutes.

2 Add the apples and poach for about 15 minutes, then allow to cool in the poaching liquid. Remove and slice the apples in half.

3 Bring the poaching liquid to a simmer and reduce until it's slightly more syrupy.

4 Place the salad leaves on a platter. Place the apples on the leaves and sprinkle with Gorgonzola and walnuts. Drizzle over a little of the syrupy poaching liquid.

KEEPING IT LOCAL: IRISH EATING APPLES IN SEASON, SUCH AS ARD CAIRN RUSSET, WORK REALLY WELL WITH THIS RECIPE AS WELL AS THE MILD WICKLOW BLUE, OUR LOCAL CHEESE.

BROAD BEAN AND PECORINO SALAD

INSALATA DI FAVE E PECORINO / SERVES 4

IN A LOVELY OLD FARMHOUSE OUTSIDE OF ROME, WHERE THE OWNER SPECIALISED IN RABBIT BREEDING, I WAS INVITED TO TASTE SOMETHING 'TRULY SPECIAL'. I BRACED MYSELF FOR '20 WAYS WITH RABBIT' ONLY TO BE TREATED TO BROAD BEANS AND PECORINO, A SEASONAL TREAT. IT'S AN UNEXPECTEDLY DELICIOUS COMBINATION.

225g broad beans
3 tbsp extra virgin olive oil
170g Pecorino, shaved or diced
100g rocket
salt and freshly ground black pepper
mint leaves, to garnish

1 Blanch the broad beans in a large saucepan of boiling water. Drain and rinse in cold running water until the beans are cold.
2 Place the beans in a serving bowl. Pour over the olive oil, then add the Pecorino and rocket and toss. Season to taste. Sprinkle mint leaves over the top and serve.

 KEEPING IT LOCAL: BROAD BEANS GROW SO WELL HERE. TRY THEM WITH A KNOCKALARA FARMHOUSE CHEESE AND RAPESEED OIL.

SORREL FLAN

CROSTATA DI ACETOSELLA / SERVES 6-8

I LIKE TO USE FRESH BABY SORREL LEAVES STIRRED INTO MASHED POTATOES OR SHREDDED INTO A MIXED SALAD. I USE THE OLDER LEAVES FOR SOUP, BUT ONE TIP I CAN SHARE WITH YOU IS TO DISCARD THE STALKS, AS THEY CAN BE VERY STRINGY WHEN OLDER.

FOR THE PASTRY:
200g plain flour, plus extra for dusting
120g butter, chilled and diced
1 egg yolk
2-3 tbsp chilled water (you may need less)

FOR THE FILLING:
2 large eggs + 2 egg yolks
50g sorrel, finely shredded
150ml cream
100g crème fraîche
pinch of nutmeg
salt and freshly ground black pepper
100g grated Fontina cheese

1 Sieve the flour into a mixing bowl. Add the butter and rub it into the flour until the mixture resembles breadcrumbs.

2 Add the egg yolk and the water and mix to form a dough. Wrap the dough in cling film and allow to rest in the fridge for 30 minutes.

3 While the dough is resting, preheat the oven to 180°C/fan 160°C/gas 4. Butter a 20cm flan tin with a removable base.

4 Roll out the pastry on a floured surface until it's slightly larger than the tin. Line the tin with the pastry and trim the edges. Place a circle of baking paper over the pastry and fill with baking beans. Transfer to the oven and bake for 8 minutes. Remove the beans and paper and return to the oven for 5 minutes more.

5 To make the filling, place all the ingredients except the Fontina cheese into a large bowl and mix gently.

6 Pour the filling into the pastry case and sprinkle the Fontina cheese on top. Bake for 10–12 minutes, or until the filling is set.

KEEPING IT LOCAL: USE RAINBOW CHARD FROM THE GARDEN – IT'S EASY TO GROW AND VERY VERSATILE. TRY SAUTÉING IT WITH GARLIC AND A DRIZZLE OF OLIVE OIL FOR ANOTHER ITALIAN-STYLE DISH OR TRY A DELICIOUS LOCAL CHEDDAR INSTEAD OF THE FONTINA.

FISH & SHELLFISH

I'M ALWAYS INTRIGUED WHEN I SEE SMOKED SALMON ON A MENU IN ITALY – MY NATIONAL PRIDE COMES TO THE FORE. EVEN THOUGH I KNOW THAT SMOKED SALMON IS AVAILABLE WORLDWIDE, IT'S SOMETHING THAT I THINK OF AS INTRINSICALLY IRISH. SO BEFORE I WAX LYRICAL, LET ME TELL YOU ABOUT THE SMOKED SWORD FISH THAT'S TYPICALLY SERVED ALONGSIDE THE SALMON – IT IS TRULY DIVINE. JUST LIGHTLY SMOKED, IT TAKES ON A VERY PALE CARAMEL COLOUR, AND LIBERALLY SPRINKLED WITH SICILIAN CAPERS AND FRESH LEMONS, IT'S A MASTERPIECE.

SURROUNDED BY WATER AS WELL AS INLAND LAKES AND RIVERS, THERE IS NO SHORTAGE OF FISH IN ITALY. THE ARRAY IS WONDERFUL, FROM *BRANZINO* (A BRONZED SEA BASS) TO TUNA, FROM *BACCALÀ* (SALTED COD) TO OCTOPUS. THE LIST IS ENDLESS. FISH IS CURED, STUFFED, SMOKED, BOILED, ROASTED, BAKED, STEWED, GRILLED – AND IT'S ALL DELICIOUS AND HEALTHY.

HERE ARE A FEW OF MY FAVOURITE AND INTERESTING INGREDIENTS.

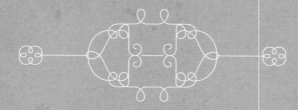

- BOTTARGA – Not far off the white truffle in price, *bottarga* is a fine Italian secret. It is the roe of the tuna (or grey mullet), which is salted, pressed and dried to preserve it and later served with lemon and olive oil as an *antipasto* or grated over a pasta plate.

- VONGOLE (clams) are important in the Italian diet, beginning with the *antipasto* and going through to the second course, my favourite being *linguine alla vongole* – simple but bursting with real flavour. You would mostly find hard-shelled ones; the Mediterranean doesn't really have anything like soft-shelled clams.

  Everyone speaks about the *vongole veraci,* which are known as carpet shell clams. They are about 5cm wide, but you will find smaller, cheaper ones that look similar but are slightly yellow. They are *vongole gialle* – yellow carpet shell clams. Clams are eaten both raw and cooked.

- TELLINE, also known as *arselle*, are known as wedge shell clams. They live in the wash zone of beaches. These are generally cooked and served with a sauce.

- CANNOLICCHI, or razor clams, have a rectangular blade like old-fashioned razors.

- COZZE are the mussels of every kind you'll see clinging in shiny black carpets to any rocky surface. Most Italian cozze are commercially raised, and the Laguna Veneta is especially well known for its cozze.

- FASOLARI are cockles and are consumed both raw and cooked.

- OCTOPUS (*POLPO*) – The smaller, the tenderer. Octopus can be prepared whole, which is a bit of a shock when served to you, as it sits head up and all eight legs sprawling. 'Where do I start?' is the first thing you think once you've ascertained that it's not looking at you! It's also delicious in a seafood stew and in a salad, but my favourite is carpaccio of octopus, served simply with a lemon and olive oil dressing. Cut very thinly, it really is quite delicate and has a soft texture.

- SEA URCHINS (*RICCI DI MARE*) – I met an Irish grandmother who travelled to Sicily to meet the new soon-to-be in-laws. They lived in a beautiful costal town and their hospitality was second to one. The Irish granny told me of the many seafood dishes prepared for her, including sea urchins. I enquired as to whether she had enjoyed them. 'Well, it was a bit difficult to enjoy something that was moving away from you across the table as you were attempting to eat it!' she replied. It was an exaggeration, but sea urchins are best eaten fresh and uncooked and are often sold by the water's edge. They are also cooked in pasta sauces, which may be more palatable to some of us.

CHARGRILLED DUBLIN BAY PRAWNS

GAMBERONI ALLA GRIGLIA /SERVES 4

BRINGING A BEAUTIFUL PLATTER OF PRAWNS TO THE TABLE IS A GREAT CROWD PLEASER. JUST MAKE SURE YOU HAVE ENOUGH FINGER BOWLS, BECAUSE THIS IS DEFINITELY A HANDS-ON EXPERIENCE!

20 large whole prawns

2 tbsp extra virgin olive oil

a little lemon juice, to drizzle

dill, to garnish

lemon wedges, to serve

FOR THE TOMATO SALSA:

3 large tomatoes, deseeded and finely diced

1 shallot, very finely chopped

1/2 lemon, zest and juice

4 tbsp extra virgin olive oil

1 tsp chopped dill

pinch of sugar

salt and freshly ground black pepper

1 To make the salsa, combine all the ingredients and set aside.
2 Preheat the BBQ. Brush the prawns with oil.
3 Grill the prawns over a direct medium heat for about 4 minutes, turning once, until cooked.
4 Place the prawns on a large serving platter and drizzle with a little lemon juice. Spoon over the salsa. Garnish with dill and serve with lemon wedges.

KEEPING IT LOCAL: WHY NOT MAKE THIS A LOCAL FEAST BY ADDING
PLATTERS OF CONNEMARA OYSTERS AND MUSSELS?

COD WITH *SALMORIGLIO*

MERLUZZO CON SALMORIGLIO / SERVES 4

SALMORIGLIO IS THE CLASSIC SICILIAN SAUCE USED FOR ROASTED MEATS AS WELL AS FISH. WE ALSO ENJOY THIS SAUCE OVER SWORDFISH IN THE SUMMER.

4 x 180g cod fillets
salt and freshly ground black pepper
extra virgin olive oil
garden salad, to serve

FOR THE *SALMORIGLIO*:
2 garlic cloves, finely chopped
4 tbsp extra virgin olive oil
2 tbsp lemon juice
2 tsp finely chopped oregano
salt and freshly ground black pepper

1 Preheat the oven to 180°C/fan 160°C/gas 4.
2 Season the fish generously with salt and freshly ground black pepper and place in a roasting pan with a little olive oil. Roast for 10–12 minutes, depending on the thickness of the cod.
3 Meanwhile, combine all the ingredients for the *salmoriglio* in a bowl and whisk vigorously.
4 Spoon the sauce over the cooked fish and serve immediately with a salad.

KEEPING IT LOCAL: THIS SAUCE IS DELICIOUS WITH OUR LOCAL HADDOCK FROM KILMORE QUAY.

SWORDFISH WITH CHILLI AND ORANGE

PESCE SPADA CON PEPERONCINO E ARANCIA / SERVES 4

WHEN I MAKE THIS DISH, I CAN'T HELP THINKING OF THE WONDERFUL CITRUS FRUITS IN THE GROVES ALONG THE SLOPES NEAR SORRENTO ON THE AMALFI COAST. THIS RECIPE BRINGS BACK ALL THOSE WONDERFUL FRAGRANCES.

4 x 180g swordfish steaks

salt and freshly ground black pepper

3 garlic cloves, finely chopped

2 red chillies, deseeded and finely chopped

1 tbsp finely chopped parsley

1 tsp chopped rosemary

4 tbsp extra virgin olive oil

2 tbsp lemon juice

200ml freshly squeezed orange juice

lemon and orange slices, to garnish

rosemary sprigs, to garnish

steamed potatoes, to serve

1 Preheat the oven to 180°C/fan 160°C/gas 4. Lightly oil a baking dish.

2 Season the swordfish steaks with salt and freshly ground black pepper.

3 Mix together the garlic, chillies, parsley, rosemary, olive oil and lemon juice. Spread the mixture on both sides of the fish steaks.

4 Arrange the fish in a single layer in the baking dish. Pour the orange juice over the fish to just cover it and bake, covered, for about 20 minutes, until the fish is opaque and firm to the touch. Transfer to a serving plate and keep warm.

5 Pour the orange juice mixture into a saucepan and simmer to reduce it (or thicken it with a little cornflour.)

6 Garnish the fish with lemon and orange slices and rosemary sprigs and spoon over the orange sauce. Serve with steamed potatoes.

  KEEPING IT LOCAL: SAUTÉED GARDEN SPINACH PLACED UNDER THE FISH WHEN IT'S IN THE OVEN MAKES A COLOURFUL LAYER. I ALSO PREPARE THIS DISH WITH LEMON SOLE TOO FOR VERY TASTY RESULTS.

SCALLOPS WITH PROSCIUTTO AND BALSAMIC GLAZE

CAPESANTE CON PROSCIUTTO E CREMA BALSAMICA / SERVES 4

EVERY TIME YOU MAKE THIS DISH YOU WILL HEAR 'WOW' AROUND THE TABLE, FOLLOWED BY SILENCE, AND THAT, MY FELLOW COOKS, IS THE SOUND OF EVERYONE ENJOYING THIS DISH.

200ml balsamic vinegar
1 tbsp brown sugar
8 thin slices prosciutto
16 large scallops
16 small rosemary sprigs
extra virgin olive oil
salt and freshly ground black pepper

1 Combine the balsamic vinegar and brown sugar in a small saucepan and bring to a boil over a moderate heat. Reduce the heat to low and simmer until the mixture has reduced by one-third. Allow to cool.
2 Meanwhile, slice each piece of prosciutto in half lengthwise and wrap around the scallops, securing each with a sprig of rosemary. Brush with olive oil and season.
3 Cook the scallops in a griddle pan over a medium heat, turning once, until they are firm to the touch and opaque in the centre. Transfer to a serving plate and drizzle with the balsamic glaze.

 KEEPING IT LOCAL: USE DRY-CURED GUBBEEN BACON TO WRAP AROUND KILMORE QUAY SCALLOPS, OR YOU MAY PREFER TO USE PRAWNS.

SEAFOOD STEW

ZUPPA DI FRUTTI DI MARE / SERVES 4

THIS IS A GIFT FROM THE SEA. LIKE ITALY, WE'RE FORTUNATE TO HAVE A WONDERFUL COASTLINE. THIS IS PRETTY FILLING, ESPECIALLY WHEN ENJOYED WITH THE BRUSCHETTA, BUT A GREEN SALAD ALONGSIDE IS LOVELY TOO.

extra virgin olive oil

1 onion, finely chopped

1 fennel bulb, chopped

1 garlic clove, chopped

1 red chilli, finely sliced

1 tbsp tomato purée

125ml white wine

400ml vegetable stock

450g monkfish, diced

400g squid, cleaned and diced

12 mussels, debearded and scrubbed well

12 prawns

salt and freshly ground black pepper

2 tbsp chopped parsley

bruschetta, to serve

1 Heat some olive oil in a large saucepan over a medium heat. Add the onion and sauté for 5 minutes, then add the fennel, garlic and chilli and cook for a further 5–6 minutes, stirring from time to time.

2 Stir in the tomato purée, add the wine and simmer for 2 minutes. Add the stock and bring to a simmer.

3 Stir in the diced monkfish, squid and mussels and cook for about 3 minutes, until the fish is firm to the touch and the mussels have opened (discard any that remain closed). Add the prawns and simmer for a further 1–2 minutes. Season to taste.

4 Sprinkle over the chopped parsley and serve with bruschetta.

KEEPING IT LOCAL: I'VE ALSO SERVED THIS WITH IRISH SODA BREAD, WHICH WORKS WELL WITH ALL FISH DISHES.

WHOLE BAKED SEA BASS WITH A RED PEPPER AND FENNEL SAUCE

SPIGOLA AL FORNO CON SALSA DI PEPERONI E FINOCCHI / SERVES 4

A WHOLE FISH IS ALWAYS AN EASY WAY TO ENTERTAIN A LARGE GROUP OF FRIENDS AND FAMILY. IN THE SUMMER I USUALLY PREPARE HEALTHY LEAFY SALADS AND ENJOY THIS DISH ALFRESCO. WELL, THERE'S ALWAYS HOPE!

FOR THE BAKED SEA BASS:

2 leeks, roughly chopped

1 onion, sliced

1 fennel bulb, sliced

1 red pepper, roughly chopped

1 x 700g sea bass, scaled, gutted and fins trimmed

3 tbsp extra virgin olive oil

salt and freshly ground black pepper

2 lemons, 1 sliced and 1 cut into wedges

FOR THE RED PEPPER AND FENNEL SAUCE:

2 tbsp extra virgin olive oil

2 onions, finely sliced

1 leek, roughly chopped

1 tbsp fennel seeds, crushed

1 red pepper, roasted, skinned and chopped

1 tbsp honey

100ml vegetable stock

1 tbsp chopped parsley

1 Preheat the oven to 180°C/fan 160°C/gas 4.

2 To make the sauce, heat the oil in a saucepan over a medium-low heat. Add the onions, leek and fennel seeds and sauté for 5–7 minutes, until the onions are softened but not browned. Add the red pepper, honey and stock. Continue to cook for a further 4 minutes. Blitz in a blender until roughly smooth and stir in the parsley. Keep warm and set aside.

3 Place the leeks, onion, most of the fennel slices and the chopped red pepper onto a sheet of foil. Place the sea bass on top, drizzle with the olive oil, sprinkle with a little salt and pepper and stuff the cavity with a few fennel and lemon slices.

4 Wrap the foil over the fish and place in the oven to cook for 25–30 minutes, checking from time to time and basting with some of the sauce.

5 Using two fish slices, transfer the fish onto a large serving platter and spoon over the sauce. Serve with lemon wedges.

 KEEPING IT LOCAL: IF FENNEL ISN'T TO YOUR LIKING, TRY SOME LOCAL COURGETTES, WHICH ARE PLENTIFUL IN THE SUMMER.

TUNA WITH WHITE BEANS AND ARTICHOKES

TONNO CON FAGIOLI E CARCIOFI / SERVES 4

PERSONALLY, I PREFER TO SIMPLY SEAR THE TUNA TO THE POINT OF MEDIUM RARE, WHICH FIRMS IT UP ON THE OUTSIDE, BUT WHEN YOU CUT INTO THE STEAK YOU EXPERIENCE A SOFT AND FLAVOURSOME MEAT.

4 x 180g tuna steaks
300g cooked cannellini beans
10 cherry tomatoes, halved
4 marinated artichoke hearts, sliced
2 shallots, finely chopped
1 tbsp chopped chives
1 tsp chopped rosemary
extra virgin olive oil

salt and freshly ground black pepper
lemon slices, to garnish
rosemary sprigs, to garnish

FOR THE MARINADE:
4 tbsp olive oil
1 lemon, zest and juice
$\frac{1}{2}$ tsp chilli flakes

1 For the marinade, combine the olive oil, lemon zest and juice with the chilli flakes. Marinade the tuna steaks in this for about half an hour, turning from time to time.
2 Meanwhile, combine the cannellini beans, tomatoes, artichoke hearts, shallots, chives and rosemary in a bowl. Drizzle over some olive oil and season to taste.
3 Heat some olive oil in a frying pan over a medium-high heat. Drain the tuna from the marinade, pat dry, season and sear in the frying pan for 2–3 minutes on each side. The tuna should still be medium soft to the touch in the centre.
4 Transfer some bean salad to each plate and place a tuna steak on top. Place a lemon slice and a sprig of rosemary on top of the tuna steak and serve.

KEEPING IT LOCAL: BLUE FIN AND ALBACORE TUNA ARE CAUGHT OFF THE COAST OF IRELAND. CONNEMARA SMOKEHOUSE PREPARES DELICIOUS COLD SMOKED TUNA AND HONEY ROAST TUNA.

POULTRY & MEAT

MEAT MAY BE ENJOYED AS A MAIN COURSE PERHAPS ONLY ONCE PER WEEK, BUT THERE IS MEAT MANY DAYS IN THE DIET IN SMALLER QUANTITIES, AS PROSCIUTTO AND SALAMI ARE SERVED AS *ANTIPASTO*, WHILE PANCETTA AND *GUANCIALE* (PIG'S CHEEK) AS WELL AS SAUSAGES AND MINCED MEATS ARE USED IN PASTA SAUCES.

MEAT IS ENJOYED MORE IN NORTHERN ITALY, WHEREAS SOUTHERN ITALY IS MORE SEAFOOD ORIENTED. IT'S GEOGRAPHICAL LOGIC. BUT IN SOUTHERN ITALY THEY HAVE THEIR PRIZED BLACK PIG, WHICH IS FED ON ACORNS AND HAZELNUTS, AND THE SALAMI MADE IN THE NEBRODI MOUNTAINS IS SIMPLY DELICIOUS. A MEAL I WILL NEVER FORGET WAS IN THE NANGALARRUNI RESTAURANT IN CASTELBUONO, WHERE THEY CELEBRATE THIS PRIZED PIG AS WELL AS FORAGED AND LOCAL FOODS IN EVERY DISH. THEIR PASTA WITH WILD BOAR RAGÙ WITH WILD MUSHROOMS IS OUTSTANDING.

Italian butchery skills are well known and the food culture is that every cut of the meat is used, whether for roasting, boiling, stewing, grilling, curing or making sausages and salami. Historically, meat was a luxury. A farmer from Bracciano once showed me how a classic pork sausage ragù was made, served with lots of polenta. She then explained that in the past, the polenta was spread out on a large wooden board and placed in the centre of the table and the ragu was placed in the centre of the board. The rule was that the children had to eat from the outside in, so they had to eat the polenta first before reaching their prize of the meat.

What I love about Italian meat dishes is the variety of flavours added and the range of cooking styles, from *saltimbocca alla Romana* (veal escalope with sage and prosciutto) to ossobucco with risotto Milanese (slow-cooked veal shin), from steak parmigiana to tripe. All meat and game are on offer – goat, deer, hare and pigeon are regional specialities in addition to the lovely lamb, pork, chicken and beef that are available everywhere.

CURED MEATS – *SALUMI*

Whether they are made from veal, beef, venison, wild boar or pork, which is the most popular, *salumi* were born out of the need to conserve meat for months.

Italian preserved meats fall into two categories: those made from whole cuts like boneless thighs and shoulders, such as *prosciutto di Parma, prosciutto coppa, culatella, mortadella* and *pancetta,* and those made from ground meat with casings, like salami and sausage.

If you have a penchant for *prosciutto di Parma,* head to the Parma hills to enjoy the month-long festival of this delicious cured meat, where the locals celebrate for the entire month of August. Prosciutto is available in two forms: *crudo* (raw) and *cotto* (cooked).

Salumi are an important part of the Italian regional kitchen. They show up as appetisers in homes and *trattorie,* or served with bread, they're perfect for an informal meal. Most cured meats arrive at the table ungarnished, while some, like *bresaola* (air-dried beef from Lombardy), are marinated with olive oil, pepper and perhaps a drizzle of lemon juice. Others, such as the *sopressata* from around Venice, which is a dry-cured salami, are stored in jars of olive oil, which is especially delicious in panini.

Historically, salami was popular among the poor in Italy because it would keep for long periods of time without refrigeration. The word 'salami' was used to refer to all kinds of cured meats.

MIXED *ANTIPASTO* PLATTER

ANTIPASTO MISTO / SERVES 4

THIS IS PRIMARILY A CHARCUTERIE PLATTER, WHICH CAN BE ENJOYED WITH AN ENDLESS LIST OF *ANTIPASTI* LIKE *CAPONATA*, SUNDRIED TOMATOES, SLICES OF GORGONZOLA, CACIOCAVALLO OR PROVOLONE, ROASTED GRAPES AND SO ON. FOR A HEALTHY OPTION, I ADD MORE SALAD LEAVES, OLIVES AND GRILLED COURGETTES.

250g marinated artichokes, drained and sliced into wedges
8 slices of prosciutto
8 slices of bresaola
8 slices of salami
8 slices of mortadella
2 red peppers, roasted and sliced
4 tbsp green olives
crusty bread, to serve
extra virgin olive oil, to serve

1 Arrange the artichokes, meats, red pepper and olives on 2 large platters or boards.
2 Serve with crusty bread and drizzle with olive oil.

 KEEPING IT LOCAL: TRY AIR-DRIED CONNEMARA LAMB, BEEF AND PORK AND SERVE WITH CARAMELISED APPLES, MINT, YOGHURT AND HORSERADISH CREAM. YUM!

SUPREME OF CHICKEN WITH ROCKET AND PARMESAN STUFFING

POLLO RIPIENO DI RUCOLA E PARMIGIANO / SERVES 4

THIS LOOKS SO ATTRACTIVE ON THE PLATE, ESPECIALLY FOR DINNER PARTIES. I HAVE INCLUDED A ROCKET OIL IN THE RECIPE – MY VERSION OF POWER JUICE AND HANDY FOR DRIZZLING ON SALADS!

4 x 200g chicken supremes (chicken breast with the wing bone attached)
extra virgin olive oil
salt and freshly ground black pepper
1 lemon, zest only
1 tsp chopped thyme

FOR THE STUFFING:
extra virgin olive oil
1 onion, finely chopped
1 tsp chopped thyme
100g cream cheese
1/2 bunch rocket, washed
4 tbsp freshly grated Parmesan
salt and freshly ground black pepper

FOR THE ROCKET OIL:
1/2 bunch rocket
extra virgin olive oil

1 Preheat the oven to 180°C/fan 160°C/gas 4.
2 To make the stuffing, heat a frying pan with some olive oil over a medium heat. Add the onion and sauté for 5–6 minutes. Add the thyme and gently cook for 1 minute. Remove from the heat and allow to cool. Stir in the cream cheese, rocket and Parmesan and season to taste.
3 Make a 'pocket' in the side of each chicken breast, then spoon in the cooled rocket stuffing. Rub each chicken breast with olive oil and sprinkle generously with salt, pepper, lemon zest and thyme.
4 Place the chicken breasts on a roasting pan and roast in the oven for 25–30 minutes, until the juices run clear (not pink) when pierced with a skewer. Baste from time to time with the pan juices.
5 In the meantime, to make the rocket oil, place the rocket in a food processor and drizzle in enough olive oil to make a loose mixture.
6 Remove the chicken from the oven and allow it to stand for about 5 minutes before serving with rocket oil drizzled over. This is delicious with honey roast vegetables in the winter and a crisp garden salad in the summer.

KEEPING IT LOCAL: IN THE WINTER, I ADD THIS STUFFING TO PHEASANT FROM MY LOCAL WILD IRISH GAME FOR A MOUTH-WATERING COMBINATION.

CHICKEN WITH PROSECCO AND SHALLOTS

POLLO CON PROSECCO E SCALOGNO / SERVES 4

AH, PROSECCO – WHERE DO I BEGIN WITH THIS WONDERFUL COMBINATION? AND THERE'S JUST ENOUGH PROSECCO LEFT IN THE BOTTLE FOR THE CHEF! THIS IS A SIMPLE AND EASY DISH TO DELIGHT YOUR FRIENDS ON A SUMMER EVENING. FOR A SWEETER VERSION OF THIS SAUCE, I HAVE OFTEN SUBSTITUTED FRESH PEACHES FOR THE PANCETTA.

2 tbsp extra virgin olive oil

3 tbsp flour, lightly seasoned with salt, freshly ground black pepper and 1 tbsp orange zest

1.4kg chicken, portioned and trimmed

150g pancetta, diced

12 small shallots, peeled and halved

1 red chilli, finely chopped

2 tsp chopped rosemary

500ml Prosecco or any dry sparkling wine

salt and freshly ground black pepper

warm red pepper and bean salad, to serve

rosemary sprigs, to garnish

1 Heat a large casserole pan with the olive oil over a medium heat. Put the seasoned flour and chicken portions into a clear plastic bag and toss until the chicken is well coated. Remove the chicken portions and brown them in batches by placing them skin side down into the pan. Transfer to a plate.

2 Add the pancetta to the pan and cook until crisp. Lower the heat and add the shallots, chilli and rosemary and sauté for about 4 minutes.

3 Return the chicken to the pan, pour over the Prosecco and allow to simmer for 20–25 minutes, until a fragrant syrupy sauce begins to form. Season to taste.

4 Check that the chicken is cooked by inserting a skewer into the thickest part of the thigh – the juices should run clear. Serve with a warm red pepper and bean salad and garnish with rosemary sprigs.

KEEPING IT LOCAL: TRY THE ARTISAN CIDER FROM THE ARMAGH CIDER COMPANY AND ADD A LITTLE CHICKEN STOCK IF YOU DON'T HAVE PROSECCO.

PANCETTA-WRAPPED CHICKEN THIGHS WITH MOZZARELLA STUFFING

COSCE DI POLLO AVVOLTI IN PANCETTA CON RIPIENO DI MOZZARELLA / SERVES 4

CHICKEN THIGHS ARE SO VERSATILE AND PACKED WITH FLAVOUR. CHICKEN BREASTS CAN DRY OUT QUITE QUICKLY IN THE COOKING PROCESS, BUT THIGHS ARE GREAT FOR LONGER COOKING AND ARE INEXPENSIVE TOO.

4 sundried tomatoes, diced

4 tbsp breadcrumbs

1 tbsp chopped parsley

$\frac{1}{2}$ lemon, zest and juice

salt and freshly ground black pepper

8 chicken thighs, bones removed and skin left on

100g buffalo mozzarella, sliced

8 basil leaves

8 slices of pancetta

extra virgin olive oil

thyme-roasted pumpkin wedges, to serve

1 Preheat the oven to 180°C/fan 160°C/gas 4.
2 Combine the sundried tomatoes, breadcrumbs, parsley, lemon zest and juice in a bowl. Season to taste.
3 Place each chicken thigh on a board. Spoon over some stuffing, place a slice of mozzarella over the stuffing and finally add a basil leaf. Roll up and wrap a slice of pancetta around each thigh, securing with a cocktail stick.
4 Place the thighs in a roasting pan drizzled with the olive oil and roast for 25–30 minutes, until golden and cooked through. Serve with thyme-roasted pumpkin wedges.

KEEPING IT LOCAL: GET YOURSELF DOWN TO TOONSBRIDGE DAIRY IN MACROOM, CO. CORK, FOR SOME REAL IRISH MOZZARELLA, MADE ON THE FARM FROM THEIR WATER BUFFALO. ALTERNATIVELY, TRY MY LOCAL ST KEVIN'S CHEESE.

SPATCHCOCK CHICKEN WITH 40 CLOVES OF GARLIC

POLLO ALLA DIAVOLA CON 40 SPICCHI DI AGLIO / SERVES 4

'WOW, ALL THAT GARLIC!' I THOUGHT THE FIRST TIME I ATE THIS, BUT THE GARLIC GETS SWEETER WHEN COOKED, SO IT ISN'T THAT POWERFUL AT ALL. THE SAUCE IS VERY CREAMY AND SMOOTH.

1.5kg chicken, spatchcocked (see instructions below or ask your butcher to do it for you)
extra virgin olive oil
8–10 small shallots, peeled and left whole
8 medium roasting potatoes, peeled and halved
40 garlic cloves, peeled
250ml chicken stock, heated
100ml white wine
1 lemon, juice only, then roughly chop the lemon
4 rosemary sprigs
3 bay leaves
salt and freshly ground black pepper
4 tbsp basil pesto (see page 75)

1 Preheat the oven to 180°C/fan 160°C/gas 4.
2 To spatchcock the chicken, remove the winglets with a scissors, then turn the chicken breast side down with the tail pointed towards you. Insert the scissors underneath the cavity and cut straight up 2cm on either side of the backbone. Remove the bone. Turn the chicken over and press down firmly, until you hear the rib bones crack. Flatten to ensure the chicken is the same thickness on both sides. To secure the chicken, insert 2 skewers crisscrossing diagonally from the breast and out the other side (inserting the skewers is optional).
3 Heat a generous amount of oil in a roasting pan by placing it in the oven for about 5 minutes. Add the spatchcocked chicken, the shallots and the potatoes and coat in the hot oil. Place in the oven for 15 minutes.

4 Add the garlic, then pour in the stock, wine and lemon juice. Add the chopped lemon to the roasting pan with the rosemary sprigs and bay leaves and season.

5 Cover with foil and return to the oven for a further 35–40 minutes, basting the chicken from time to time. Add some extra stock if the sauce is reducing too quickly. Check that the chicken is cooked by inserting a skewer into the thickest part of the thigh – the juices should run clear.

6 Remove the chicken to a serving platter and allow to rest. Keep it warm by loosely covering it with foil.

7 Meanwhile, place the roasting pan on the hob and bring the sauce to the boil. Allow it to simmer for 2–3 minutes to thicken slightly. Some of the garlic will dissolve into the sauce.

8 Combine the basil pesto with 3 tbsp olive oil to form a thin sauce.

9 Serve the chicken with the roasted potatoes and shallots. Drizzle over some of the pesto sauce and serve immediately.

KEEPING IT LOCAL: COOLANOWLE ORGANIC MEAT IN COUNTY CARLOW HAS DELICIOUS ORGANIC CHICKENS. YOU COULD ALSO TRY THIS RECIPE WITH A BUTTERFLIED LEG OF WICKLOW LAMB FROM ROBERT CULLENS IN WICKLOW TOWN.

DATE AND HAZELNUT STUFFED PORK TENDERLOIN

FILETTO DI MAIALE RIPIENO DI DATTERI E NOCCIOLE / SERVES 4-5

IN THE BAROQUE TOWN OF NOTO IN SICILY, I DISCOVERED A WONDERFUL LITTLE RESTAURANT THAT SERVED PORK WITH A FIG AND HAZELNUT STUFFING AND IT WAS HEAVENLY. MY FAMILY PREFERS THE TEXTURE OF DATES, SO HERE IS THE FULVIO FAVOURITE.

2 x 350g pork tenderloins

FOR THE STUFFING:

2 tbsp extra virgin olive oil

1 onion, finely chopped

8 dates, pitted and chopped

5 tbsp breadcrumbs

3 tbsp toasted, chopped hazelnuts

$1/2$ tsp chopped oregano

FOR THE SAUCE:

100ml white wine

100ml cream

$1/2$ tsp chopped oregano

salt and freshly ground black pepper

1 Preheat the oven to 180°C/fan 160°C/gas 4.

2 To make the stuffing, heat a frying pan with the olive oil over a low heat. Sauté the onion for 7–8 minutes, then add the dates and cook for a further 3 minutes. Stir in the breadcrumbs, hazelnuts and oregano, then remove from the heat and allow to cool.

3 Slice the tenderloins through the centre but not all the way through and spoon in the stuffing. Do not overfill. Replace the top half of the tenderloin.

4 Place the stuffed tenderloins in a roasting pan and drizzle with a little olive oil. Roast for 25–30 minutes, turning once or twice. Allow to rest for 10 minutes before slicing.

5 Meanwhile, to make the sauce, combine the white wine, cream and oregano in a small saucepan and simmer for 2–3 minutes. Add seasoning to taste and keep warm.

6 Serve the sliced tenderloin with the oregano cream sauce drizzled over.

KEEPING IT LOCAL: PREPARE THE STUFFING WITH CARAMELISED AUTUMNAL EATING APPLES LIKE GOLDEN PIPPIN AND SERVE WITH A CREAM AND CIDER SAUCE USING A LOCAL APPLE CIDER.

ITALIAN WEDDING SOUP

ZUPPA NUZIALE / SERVES 4

THIS IS TRADITIONALLY AN ITALIAN-AMERICAN SOUP. WEDDING SOUP IS APPARENTLY A MISTRANSLATION FROM THE ITALIAN *MINESTRA MARITATA*, WHICH REFERS TO ALL THE GREEN VEGETABLES AND MEAT THAT 'MARRY' TOGETHER. THAT SAID, IT'S A DELICIOUS RECIPE FOR SUPPER AND A VERY ENERGISING SOUP.

FOR THE MEATBALLS:

400g lean pork, minced

50g fresh breadcrumbs

1 garlic clove, chopped

2 tsp wholegrain mustard

1/2 tsp chopped oregano

1 egg, beaten

salt and freshly ground black pepper

extra virgin olive oil

FOR THE SOUP:

2 tbsp extra virgin olive oil

2 onions, finely chopped

2 celery stalks, chopped

1.2 litres chicken stock

125ml white wine

50g orzo pasta

2 tbsp chopped dill

50g baby spinach leaves, washed and trimmed

Parmesan shavings, to garnish

1 For the meatballs, combine the pork mince, breadcrumbs, garlic, mustard, oregano, egg, salt and freshly ground black pepper in a large bowl. Mix well. Fry a tiny piece and check for seasoning, adjusting the main mixture if required. Using wet hands, roll the mixture into 20 small meatballs.

2 Heat some olive oil in a frying pan over a medium heat. Sauté the meatballs for about 6–7 minutes, until cooked through. Set aside.

3 In the meantime, to make the soup, heat the olive oil in a large saucepan over a medium heat. Add the onions and celery and sauté for 5–6 minutes, until softened but not browned. Add the chicken stock and wine and bring to the boil. Add the pasta to the soup and cook for 6–7 minutes. Stir in the dill and meatballs and heat through.

4 Add in the spinach and when it's just wilted, ladle into warm soup bowls and serve with a few Parmesan shavings.

KEEPING IT LOCAL: REPLACE THE MEATBALLS WITH SOME OF MCGETTIGAN'S BUTCHERS' AWARD-WINNING LAMB, ROSEMARY AND PLUM OR RHUBARB AND GINGER SAUSAGES. DELICIOUS AND INTERESTING.

SPARE RIBS WITH POLENTA CHIPS

COSTINE CON PATATINE DI POLENTA / SERVES 4

THIS IS ONE OF THOSE GREAT RECIPES THAT LOOK FANTASTIC IN THE CENTRE OF THE DINING TABLE AS HANDS RACE IN TO GRAB THE GOODIES.

12 pork spare ribs, cut into 4 sections or individually cut

extra virgin olive oil

polenta chips, to serve (see page 49)

sea salt

FOR THE MARINADE:

200ml balsamic vinegar

1 large chilli, finely chopped

3 tbsp brown sugar

1 tbsp tomato purée

2 tsp paprika

1 Place all the marinade ingredients in a saucepan and bring to the boil. Reduce the heat and simmer for 10 minutes, until it thickens. Allow to cool.

2 Coat the ribs with the marinade and leave for at least 3 hours.

3 Preheat the oven to 160°C/fan 140°C/gas 3.

4 Drizzle a large roasting pan with a little olive oil. Place the ribs in the pan and cook in the oven for about 1 hour 10 minutes, checking and basting every 15 minutes. You can also BBQ the ribs over a low to medium heat for 30–40 minutes, depending on their size, basting and checking every 10 minutes.

5 Once the ribs are cooked, leave them to rest for a few minutes, then cut into individual ribs and serve with the polenta chips. Sprinkle a few sea salt flakes over the top to serve.

KEEPING IT LOCAL: TRY HICKS BUTCHERS OF DUN LAOGHAIRE FOR WONDERFUL PORK RIBS. YOU COULD ALSO SERVE THESE WITH A MIX OF HONEY-GLAZED PARSNIP AND POTATO WEDGES.

HERB-WRAPPED FILLET OF BEEF WITH WILD MUSHROOM SAUCE

FILETTO DI MANZO AVVOLTO NELLE ERBE CON SALSA DI FUNGHI SELVATICI / SERVES 6

ALTHOUGH I LOVE TO ADD WILD MUSHROOMS TO RECIPES, I'M VERY CAREFUL WHEN FORAGING FOR THEM – 'IF IN DOUBT, JUST DON'T COOK WITH THEM' IS MY MOTTO.

extra virgin olive oil

1kg beef fillet, trimmed

salt and freshly ground black pepper

6 long parsley sprigs

6 long rosemary sprigs

6 long thyme sprigs

FOR THE WILD MUSHROOM SAUCE:

2 tbsp extra virgin olive oil

200g wild field mushrooms, roughly sliced, if required

2 garlic cloves, finely chopped

100ml white wine

200ml cream

100ml vegetable or chicken stock

salt and freshly ground black pepper

2 tbsp chopped flat-leaf parsley

purple sprouting broccoli and caramelised endive or
   chicory wedges, to serve

1 Preheat the oven to 190°C/fan 170°C/gas 5.
2 Rub some olive oil on the beef and season with salt and pepper. Rub oil over the herbs too, then lay the herbs lengthwise along the fillet and secure with kitchen string.
3 Heat some oil in a large frying pan over a high heat. Sear the fillet on all sides to colour. Using tongs, transfer to a roasting pan drizzled with oil.
4 Roast the meat in the oven for about 30 minutes, depending on how you like your beef served. Allow to stand for 10 minutes before carving.
5 In the meantime, to make the sauce, add the olive oil to the same pan the beef was cooked in. Add the mushrooms and garlic and sauté on a high heat for about 4 minutes, stirring constantly. Pour in the wine and simmer for about 3 minutes. Stir in the cream and stock, simmer for 2 minutes and season to taste. Stir in the parsley. Serve with purple sprouting broccoli and caramelised endive or chicory wedges.

KEEPING IT LOCAL: WE HAVE A GREAT COMMUNITY OF ANGUS BREEDERS HERE IN WICKLOW, SO I HAVE TO PAY HOMAGE TO THEM FOR THEIR GOOD ANIMAL CARE AND LOVE OF THE LAND. MUSHROOMS GROW WELL IN FIELDS USED FOR GRAZING COWS – AGAIN, BE CAREFUL WHAT YOU PICK.

LAMB STEW WITH LEMON AND OLIVES

SPEZZATINO DI AGNELLO CON LIMONE E OLIVE / SERVES 4-6

THIS IS AN EASY, SLOW-COOKING OVEN-TO-TABLE DISH THAT FREES YOU UP TO GET ON WITH OTHER THINGS OR EVEN SIT DOWN AND HAVE A LITTLE GLASS OF WINE! TRY TOPPING WITH SOME CROUTONS TOSSED IN LEMON ZEST AND ROSEMARY.

3 tbsp extra virgin olive oil

1.2kg shoulder of lamb, trimmed and diced into 3cm pieces

3 tbsp flour seasoned with salt and freshly ground black pepper

3 celery stalks, diced

1 onion, chopped

2 tsp chopped rosemary

salt and freshly ground black pepper

2 garlic cloves, thinly sliced

400g tinned chopped tomatoes

200ml white wine

200ml chicken stock

1 tsp caster sugar

12 green olives, pitted

zest of 1 lemon and juice of $\frac{1}{2}$

1 tbsp chopped parsley

1 Preheat the oven to 160°C/fan 140°C/gas 3.

2 Heat the oil in a large casserole over a high heat. Toss the lamb in the seasoned flour, shaking off any excess, then brown the lamb in batches and set aside on a plate.

3 Add the celery, onion, rosemary and some salt and pepper and cook on a low heat for 10 minutes, stirring from time to time. Add the garlic and cook for 1 minute, followed by the tomatoes, wine, stock and sugar. Return the meat to the casserole.

4 Cover the casserole and place in the oven for about 2 hours, stirring from time to time.

5 Stir in the olives and lemon juice. Check for seasoning and sprinkle over the lemon zest and parsley.

KEEPING IT LOCAL: BEING A WICKLOW LASS AND FROM A FAMILY OF LAMB FARMERS, I HAVE TO RECOMMEND USING WICKLOW LAMB. A GOOD TIME TO MAKE THIS DISH IS LATE SUMMER AND AUTUMN, WHEN THE LAMB IS PLENTIFUL AND FULL OF SUMMER FLAVOUR. AT THIS POINT, WE SAY THAT OUR LAMB IS HEATHER HONEY LAMB.

PISTACHIO AND FIG CRUSTED RACK OF LAMB WITH TAPENADE

CARRÈ DI AGNELLO IN CROSTA DI PISTACCHI E FICHI CON TAPENADE / SERVES 4-6

INSTEAD OF USING THE TRADITIONAL MINT SAUCE, I LIKE TO SERVE THIS SCRUMPTIOUS FIG TAPENADE WITH THE RACK OF LAMB. ASK YOUR CRAFT BUTCHER TO PREPARE THE RACK FOR YOU.

3 or 4 racks of lamb (2 cutlets per person)
extra virgin olive oil
salt and freshly ground black pepper

FOR THE FIG AND OLIVE TAPENADE:
10 dried figs, chopped
100ml water
5 anchovies, drained

4 tbsp black olives, pitted
2 tbsp roughly chopped pistachios
1 ½ tbsp capers, drained
1 tbsp honey
2 tsp wholegrain mustard
1 lemon, juice only
½ orange, zest only
125ml extra virgin olive oil

freshly ground black pepper

FOR THE CRUST:
4 dried figs, finely chopped
4 tbsp finely chopped pistachios
1 tbsp honey
1 tbsp balsamic vinegar

rosemary roast potatoes, to serve

1   Preheat the oven to 180°C/fan 160°C/gas 4.
2   To prepare the tapenade, place the figs and water in a small saucepan and simmer for 10–12 minutes, until the figs are tender. Drain and set aside.
3   Place the anchovies, pitted olives, pistachios, capers, honey, mustard, lemon juice, orange zest and cooked figs in a food processor and blend to a thick paste. With the motor still running, pour the olive oil through the feed tube in a thin, steady stream to make a thick spread. Season to taste with freshly ground black pepper only and set aside for serving later.
4   For the crust, combine all the topping ingredients and mix well. Spread over the rack of lamb, pressing down firmly (you can leave it to set in the fridge for 1 hour).
5   Place the lamb in a roasting pan. Drizzle with olive oil and season with salt and pepper.
6   Roast in the oven for 25–30 minutes, depending on the size of the rack, basting from time to time with olive oil. Allow the meat to rest for 10 minutes before slicing the lamb cutlets.
7   Place 2 cutlets on a serving plate, accompanied by the fig tapenade and rosemary roast potatoes.

 KEEPING IT LOCAL: KILLOWEN RASPBERRY YOGHURT WITH A LITTLE HONEY AND FINELY CHOPPED ROSEMARY OR MINT IS GREAT WITH THIS DISH. IT SOUNDS STRANGE, BUT IT'S DELICIOUS.

SWEETS

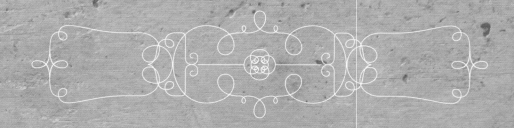

FRUIT IN SEASON IS GENERALLY DESSERT IN ITALY,
WHICH IS ALWAYS WELCOME AFTER THE RICHNESS OF
THE *ANTIPASTI, PRIMI* AND *SECONDI* COURSES. BUT FOR
SUNDAY LUNCH, ENTERTAINING AND SPECIAL OCCASIONS,
A DESSERT OR A CELEBRATION CAKE IS PRODUCED FOR
THE COFFEE COURSE.

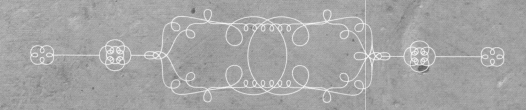

CELEBRATION CAKES

The cake course at the end of a meal is in itself a celebration. The ritual of the presentation of the cake and the discussion based exclusively on admiring this beautiful piece is a sight to behold. It's pretty unusual to bake these celebration cakes at home – they're nearly always purchased at the *pasticerria* (which, by the way, is not part of a bakery (*panifico*), as cakes are a speciality in themselves).

When it comes to presenting celebration cakes, the Italians have true style. Not only are the cakes themselves a feast for the eyes, but the packaging reaches the dizzy heights of glittering gold or sliver lettering embossed on pretty soft mint green or baby pink boxes, lavishly wrapped in sparkly cellophane, and as a gesture for the grand finale, secured with a huge bow encircling a pretty dried flower arrangement. Now that's chic!

Panettone is the most famous of Italian cakes. This is the sweet bread originally from Milan, which is served at Christmas and the New Year, but some of us could eat it all year round! We like to serve it with my version of *crèma di mascarpone* or a tipple of amaretto.

Cassata, which is traditionally Sicilian, is a more complex cake with layers of liqueur-soaked Génoise sponge cake, elaborately decorated with marzipan fruits. Today it is very elegant and one would only have a very thin slice. The beautifully coloured marzipan fruits are themselves a work of art.

Panforte, native to Sienna, dates back to the 1300s. It's a spicy Italian fruit cake with nuts, candied citrus, honey and even pepper. It was paid to the monks and nuns as a tax. It's pretty rich and is a great alternative to tax!

ALMOND CAKE

TORTA DI MANDORLE / SERVES 8

THIS IS ONE OF MY FAVOURITES. THE LIGHTLY TOASTED ALMONDS MAKE THIS A REAL WINNER FOR ME AND I'M SURE THE HEALTH BENEFITS OF THE NUTS COUNTERACT THE BUTTER AND SUGAR!

120g butter, softened, plus a little extra for greasing
220g caster sugar
4 egg yolks
180g ground almonds, plus extra for dusting the tin
70g plain flour
2 tsp baking powder
60ml milk
1 orange, zest and juice
icing sugar, for dusting
edible flowers, to decorate

1 Preheat the oven to 180°C/fan 160°C/gas 4. Butter the base and sides of a 23cm springform tin and dust with some ground almonds.
2 Whisk the butter and sugar together in a large bowl until pale and creamy. Add the egg yolks one at a time, whisking until the mixture is fluffy. Fold in the ground almonds, flour and baking powder. Stir in the milk and the orange zest and juice to form a soft batter.
3 Pour the cake mix into the springform tin and bake for 35–40 minutes, until golden. To test, insert a skewer – when it comes out clean, it's ready to be transferred to a cooling rack. Allow the cake to settle in the tin for 10–15 minutes before taking it out.
4 Dust with a little icing sugar and decorate with edible flowers.

 KEEPING IT LOCAL: HERE AT BALLYKNOCKEN, OUR HERB GARDEN IS BURSTING THROUGH ITS BOX HEDGING IN THE SUMMER, SO THIS IS WHEN I ADD SHREDDED LEMON BALM TO THE CAKE AND MAKE A LEMON BALM SYRUP TO DRIZZLE OVER THE TOP. SERVE WITH PEPPERMINT TEA ON A HOT SUMMER DAY.

HAZELNUT CAKE (SEE P.183)

CHOCOLATE BREADCRUMB AND ALMOND CAKE

TORTA DI CIOCCOLATO, PANGRATTATO E MANDORLE / SERVES 8

THIS RECIPE IS A LITTLE UNUSUAL BUT VERY SCRUMPTIOUS AND IT LOOKS PRETTY IMPRESSIVE AS A CELEBRATORY CAKE WITH STRAWBERRIES AND RASPBERRIES PILED ON TOP AND EDIBLE FLOWERS AROUND THE EDGE.

140g stale breadcrumbs, plus 1 tbsp for dusting

300ml milk

200g 70% cocoa content dark chocolate

80g butter

5 eggs, separated

180g caster sugar

100g ground almonds

cocoa powder, for dusting

chocolate shavings, to decorate

1 Preheat the oven to 180°C/fan 160°C/gas 4. Butter a 20cm round springform tin and dust with 1 tbsp of breadcrumbs.

2 Place the breadcrumbs in a large bowl. Heat the milk until it's just boiling and pour over the breadcrumbs. Allow to soak for 10 minutes.

3 Meanwhile, melt the chocolate and butter over a bain marie (a heatproof bowl set over a pot of simmering water).

4 In a large bowl, whisk the egg yolks and gradually add the sugar, whisking until the mixture is light and fluffy. Fold in the melted chocolate and butter mixture and add the soaked breadcrumbs and the ground almonds.

5 In a spotlessly clean, dry bowl, whisk the eggs whites to the stiff peak stage, then fold into the chocolate breadcrumb mixture.

6 Pour into the prepared tin and bake for 30–35 minutes, until set. The texture of this cake is fairly moist. Allow to cool in the tin for 15 minutes, then transfer to a cooling rack.

7 When cooled, place on a serving platter, dust with cocoa powder and decorate with chocolate shavings.

KEEPING IT LOCAL: USE TRADITIONAL CHURNED BUTTER SUCH AS GLENILEN FARM BUTTER FROM THE KINGSTON FAMILY AT YOUR LOCAL MARKET OR SPECIALIST FOOD SHOP.

CHOCOLATE RICOTTA TART

TORTA DI RICOTTA AL CIOCCOLATO / SERVES 8

THERE IS A GREAT ITALIAN ELEGANCE ABOUT THIS DESSERT AND IT WILL STAND PROUD AT ANY DINNER PARTY.
THE USE OF RICOTTA IN THE FILLING BRINGS A LIGHTNESS TO THIS OTHERWISE RICH DESSERT. INSTEAD OF THE
CANDIED PEEL, SOMETIMES I USE CHOPPED TOASTED HAZELNUTS.

FOR THE PASTRY:

250g plain flour

1 tbsp cocoa powder

4 tbsp caster sugar

130g butter, chilled and diced

4 tbsp Marsala or water

FOR THE FILLING:

85g caster sugar

2 egg yolks

375g ricotta cheese

1 lemon, zest only

4 tbsp dark chocolate chips

3 tbsp chopped candied peel

2 tbsp amaretto

egg wash, for brushing

1 Preheat the oven to 200°C/fan 180°C/gas 6. Butter a 30cm loose-bottomed tart tin.

2 For the pastry, sieve the flour and cocoa into a bowl, then stir in the sugar. Rub in the butter using your fingertips until the mixture resembles breadcrumbs, then work in the Marsala to make a firm dough. Wrap in cling film and refrigerate until required.

3 To make the filling, beat the sugar and egg yolks in a bowl until well incorporated, then beat in the ricotta and mix thoroughly. Stir in the lemon zest, chocolate chips, candied peel and amaretto.

4 Roll out three-quarters of the pastry on a lightly floured surface. Transfer the pastry to the prepared tin. Pour the ricotta mixture into the pastry case and level the surface.

5 Roll out the remaining pastry and cut into strips. Arrange these in a lattice over the pie. Lightly brush with the egg wash.

6 Bake for 10–12 minutes. Lower the oven to 180°C/fan 160°C/gas 4 and cook for a further 25–30 minutes, until golden and set.

7 Cool the tart in the tin. Serve at room temperature.

 KEEPING IT LOCAL: TRY THE YUMMY YEATS COUNTRY SOFT CHEESE, MADE IN DONEGAL –
IT'S RICHER THAN THE RICOTTA BUT WORKS VERY WELL IN THE RECIPE.

FRESH FRUIT TART

CROSTATA DI FRUTTA FRESCA / SERVES 8

DEFINITELY ONE OF MY FIVE A DAY! THIS IS A GREAT TART FOR DINNER PARTIES AS THE ARRANGEMENT OF FRUITS CAN ALWAYS BE CHANGED DEPENDING ON WHAT'S AVAILABLE. FOR EXAMPLE, GRAPES AND MELON WORK WELL TOGETHER. ADD A FEW FINELY CHOPPED HAZELNUTS TO THE PASTRY FOR EXTRA TEXTURE. (SEE PICTURE ON P. 55.)

FOR THE SHORTCRUST PASTRY:
225g plain flour
125g butter, chilled and diced
80g caster sugar
2 egg yolks
1 tsp vanilla extract

FOR THE FILLING:
250g mascarpone
250ml double cream
1 orange, zest only
4 tbsp caster sugar
200g strawberries, washed, hulled and halved
200g blueberries, washed
200g raspberries, washed
mint leaves, to decorate

1 Preheat the oven to 180°C/fan 160°C/gas 4. Butter a fluted 23cm loose-bottomed tart tin.

2 Place the flour, butter and sugar into a food processor and blend until it resembles fine breadcrumbs. (Alternatively, sieve the flour into a bowl, then stir in the sugar and rub in the butter using your fingertips.) Add the egg yolks and vanilla and blend for no more than 30 seconds, until the dough comes together.

3 Tip the dough out onto a floured surface and knead lightly. Refrigerate to rest, if soft. Then roll out and line the tin with the pastry. Place in the fridge for 10 minutes, then bake blind for about 15 minutes, until golden. Remove from the oven and allow to cool, then remove from the tin and transfer to a serving platter.

4 To make the filling, combine the mascarpone and cream until smooth, then add the orange zest and sugar. Spread the filling over the base. Arrange the strawberries, blueberries and raspberries over the filling and decorate with mint leaves.

KEEPING IT LOCAL: POACHED GOOSEBERRIES AND BLACKCURRANTS MACERATED IN ELDERFLOWER SYRUP ARE DELICIOUS ARRANGED ON TOP OF THIS TART. AND ELDERFLOWERS ARE FREE!

LEMON AND *PANETTONE* TRIFLE

ZUPPA INGLESE DI LIMONE E PANETTONE / SERVES 4-6

THERE ALWAYS SEEMS TO BE SOME PANETTONE LEFT OVER, DELICIOUS AS IT IS. IT CAN DRY OUT, SO THIS IS A GOOD WAY TO USE IT WITH SWEET RESULTS. WHEN POACHING THE PEARS, TRY ADDING A FEW PIECES OF LEMON ZEST. IT NOT ONLY GIVES A WONDERFUL FLAVOUR TO THE STOCK SYRUP, BUT HELPS TO KEEP THE PEARS FROM DISCOLOURING.

3 pears, peeled, cored and sliced into wedges

100g caster sugar

400ml water

100g mascarpone

120ml natural yoghurt

120ml cream

1 lemon, zest only

5 tbsp icing sugar

100ml poaching syrup from the pears

3 tbsp amaretto

8–10 slices of panettone

2 tbsp chopped pistachio nuts, plus extra to decorate

white chocolate shavings to decorate

1 To poach the pears, heat the sugar and water in a saucepan until the sugar has dissolved. Add the pears and simmer for about 15 minutes, until cooked through. Set aside.
2 Lightly whip the mascarpone, yoghurt, cream, lemon zest and icing sugar together in a bowl.
3 In a separate bowl, combine the poaching syrup and amaretto.
4 Layer a few slices of pear in pretty glasses or a large trifle bowl and spoon over the lemon yoghurt cream. Add a layer of panettone, drizzle over some of the amaretto poaching liquid and sprinkle over a few nuts. Continue layering, ending with the yoghurt mascarpone cream.
5 Decorate with pear slices, white chocolate shavings and a few nuts.

 KEEPING IT LOCAL: SELECT A FEW GREAT-LOOKING CONFERENCE PEARS AT THE MARKET STAND TO POACH IN COISREAL LONGUEVILLE, A DELICIOUS CRISP WHITE WINE FROM THE O'CALLAGHAN FAMILY IN LONGUEVILLE HOUSE, CORK.

GRANDMA'S PINE NUT CUSTARD PIE

TORTE DELLA NONNA / SERVES 8

THIS IS A TART THAT EVERY TUSCAN GRANDMOTHER PREPARES USING HER OWN UNIQUE RECIPE. IN MY OPINION, IT'S ALL ABOUT A DELICATE PASTRY AND THE SMOOTH SILKINESS OF THE FILLING WITH A PINE NUT CRUNCH ON TOP.

FOR THE PASTRY:
125g butter, softened
80g golden caster sugar
1 egg yolk
1 orange, zest only
1 tsp vanilla extract

220g plain flour
1 egg, beaten

FOR THE CUSTARD FILLING:
120g golden caster sugar
5 egg yolks
1 tsp vanilla extract

5 tbsp plain flour
700ml milk

4–6 tbsp pine nuts, for the topping
icing sugar, to decorate

1 Generously butter a 25cm deep, fluted, loose-bottomed tart tin and dust with flour.
2 To make the pastry, cream the butter and sugar in a large bowl, using an electric whisk, until light and fluffy. Beat in the egg yolk, orange zest and vanilla extract and then stir in the flour. Transfer to a lightly floured work surface and knead gently until smooth. Wrap in cling film and place in the fridge for at least 30 minutes.
3 Preheat the oven to 180°C/fan 160°C/gas 4.
4 Roll out the pastry and line the tin, then place in the fridge for 10 minutes. Line with parchment paper and fill with baking beans. Bake for about 15 minutes, until golden. Set aside.
5 To use the excess pastry, roll out and cut with a shaped cutter. Place the pastry shapes on a baking tray lined with parchment paper and brush with some beaten egg. Bake for 7–8 minutes, until just golden. Remove from the oven and allow to cool.
6 Meanwhile, to make the custard, whisk the sugar with the egg yolks and vanilla extract in a large bowl, then whisk in the flour. Warm the milk in a large saucepan until it's just below boiling point. Add the milk to the egg mixture very slowly, whisking all the time. Return the mixture to the saucepan and gently simmer until a thick custard has formed. Allow to cool slightly, then fill the tart.
7 Sprinkle over the pine nuts and bake in the oven for 15–20 minutes, until just set.
8 Leave to cool completely, then place the little pastry shapes on the edge of the tart. Dust with icing sugar and serve.

 KEEPING IT LOCAL: YOU CAN'T BEAT LOCAL RASPBERRIES IN THE SUMMER! PLACE THESE ON TOP INSTEAD OF THE PINE NUTS. MY CHILDREN THEN CALL IT *TORTA DELLA MAMMA!*

HAZELNUT CAKE WITH ORANGE CINNAMON TOPPING

TORTE DI NOCCIOLE / SERVES 8

YOUR NEIGHBOURS WILL SURPRISE YOU WITH A VISIT WHEN THEY CATCH THE AROMA OF THIS LOVELY MOIST HAZELNUT CAKE BAKING. THE SMELLS WAFTING OUT YOUR KITCHEN WINDOW ARE INTOXICATING. WHISKING THE EGG WHITES SEPARATELY AND FOLDING THEM IN GIVES THIS CAKE AN UNEXPECTED LIGHTNESS. (SEE PICTURE ON P. 175.)

220g hazelnuts, toasted, skinned and
  roughly chopped
120g butter, melted
1 tsp baking powder
1 tsp cinnamon
5 eggs, separated

185g golden caster sugar
1 tsp vanilla

FOR THE ORANGE CINNAMON TOPPING:
200g icing sugar, sieved
200g butter, softened

200g cream cheese, softened
2 oranges, zest only
1/2 tsp cinnamon (more if you prefer)

1 orange, zest only, to decorate
cinnamon sticks, to decorate

1 Preheat the oven to 170°C/fan 150°C/gas 3. Butter the sides and line the base of a 20cm springform tin with parchment paper.

2 Grind the hazelnuts in a food processor until fairly fine. Remove and place in a bowl. Add the melted butter, baking powder and cinnamon to the hazelnuts.

3 Beat the egg yolks in a bowl, then add the sugar and continue to beat until thick and pale. Add to the ground hazelnuts and fold to combine.

4 Whisk the egg whites in a spotlessly clean, dry bowl with a clean mixer until stiff. Fold into the hazelnut mixture along with the vanilla.

5 Pour the hazelnut mixture into the tin. Bake for 35–40 minutes, until golden or until an inserted skewer comes out clean. Leave in the tin for 5 minutes, then transfer onto a rack to cool completely.

6 In the meantime, prepare the topping. Cream the icing sugar and butter together until light and creamy. Fold in the cream cheese, orange zest and cinnamon and beat until smooth. Chill in the fridge for about 20 minutes.

7 Slice the cake in two and spread the topping over half of the cake. Top with the other cake half and spread the remaining topping over. Decorate with orange zest and cinnamon sticks and serve.

KEEPING IT LOCAL: FOR AN AUTUMNAL TWIST, PICK BLACKBERRIES FROM THE HEDGEROW AND ADD THE SMALLER, LESS JUICY ONES TO THE CAKE MIX. KEEP THE PLUMP, FRUITY ONES TO DECORATE THE TOP OF THE CAKE.

PANETTONE

SERVES 8

I HAD THE PLEASURE OF BEING TAUGHT HOW TO MAKE PANETTONE FROM THE FIASCONARO BROTHERS, MASTER BAKERS IN THE TOWN OF CASTELBUONO, SICILY. THEIR CAKES HAVE TRULY GONE INTO ORBIT, AS THEY HAVE SUPPLIED TO NASA IN THE PAST. THIS IS MY SIMPLER VERSION OF THIS BEAUTIFUL CAKE.

150ml milk, warmed

2 tsp dried yeast

100g golden caster sugar

3 eggs, beaten

175g butter, melted

3 tbsp Marsala

1 tsp vanilla extract

500g plain flour, plus extra for dusting

½ tsp salt

150g raisins

4 tbsp orange juice or brandy

75g candied peel

TO GLAZE:

1 egg, beaten

2 tbsp flaked almonds

1 Place the milk and yeast in a small bowl and whisk together.

2 Whisk the sugar and eggs together in a bowl until well incorporated and light, then add in the melted butter, Marsala and vanilla.

3 Place the flour and salt into a mixer fitted with a dough hook. Add in the yeast and milk mixture along with the egg mixture and knead for 5 minutes on a low speed. Cover and leave to rise in a warm, draught-free place until it doubles in size, which will take about 2 hours.

4 Meanwhile, soak the raisins in the orange juice or brandy in a small bowl.

5 Preheat the oven to 180°C/fan 160°C/gas 4. Butter and line a 20cm deep cake tin. Make a 10cm collar with double thickness parchment paper and line the sides of the tin.

6 Tip the dough out on a floured surface, mix in the raisins and candied peel and lightly knead for 3–4 minutes. The dough should be soft, so oil your hands well to handle it. Roll the dough into a ball and place it into the tin. Leave it to rise for 30 minutes.

7 Brush the top with the beaten egg and sprinkle over the almonds. Bake for about 55 minutes, or until well risen and golden. Transfer to a cooling rack.

 KEEPING IT LOCAL: AN IRISH BARM BRACK MADE WITH YEAST IS NOT UNLIKE A PANETTONE, THOUGH THERE IS MORE BUTTER AND SOMETIMES QUITE A BIT OF ALCOHOL IN PANETTONE. BUT BOTH SHOULD BE LIGHT AS COTTON WOOL WHEN MADE PROPERLY.

PANFORTE DI SIENA

SERVES 6

MEANING 'STRONG BREAD', THIS CENTURIES-OLD FESTIVE SWEET AND STICKY CAKE IS ALWAYS POPULAR. ADD A FEW CHOPPED DATES IF YOU PREFER FEWER NUTS. YOU COULD ALSO REPLACE THE FIGS WITH 100G CRANBERRIES. SERVE VERY SMALL PORTIONS OF THIS DELICIOUS TREAT, AS IT IS SO RICH.

100g almonds, roughly chopped

70g hazelnuts, roughly chopped

60g pistachio nuts, roughly chopped

60g candied orange peel, chopped

4 dried figs, chopped

100g plain flour

2 tbsp cocoa powder

$^1/_2$ tsp ground cinnamon

$^1/_2$ tsp ground nutmeg

$^1/_4$ tsp ground cloves

150g caster sugar

6 tbsp clear honey

4 tbsp icing sugar, to decorate

1 Preheat the oven to 150°C/fan 130°C/gas 2. Line a 20cm square cake tin with parchment paper.

2 Mix the nuts with the orange peel and figs in a small bowl.

3 Sieve the flour, cocoa and spices together in a large bowl and stir in the nut mixture.

4 Gently heat the sugar and honey in a pan and stir until the sugar has dissolved. Increase the heat and cook for a further 1–2 minutes.

5 Quickly stir the syrup through the dry ingredients. Spoon the mixture into the prepared cake tin, pressing it in with your fingers.

6 Bake in the oven for 30–35 minutes, until set. Allow it to cool in the tin, then remove the paper and dust with icing sugar.

KEEPING IT LOCAL: WHEN I'M MAKING MY IRISH CHRISTMAS CAKE, I NEARLY ALWAYS HAVE SPICES, FRUIT AND NUTS LEFT OVER, SO I MAKE A *PANFORTE* SO THAT THE ITALIAN SIDE OF THE FAMILY CAN HAVE A MERRY CHRISTMAS TOO. I'M ALSO PARTIAL TO SOAKING THE FIGS IN STOUT – TOTALLY NOT TRADITIONAL, BUT I LIKE THE EDGE ON THE FLAVOUR.

TORRONE

MAKES ABOUT 200G

THIS SINGS OF SICILIAN INGREDIENTS – HONEY, ALMONDS AND LEMONS. THE FIASCONARO BROTHERS, WHO EXCEL AT MAKING *TORRONE*, HAVE BEEN WELCOMED INTO THE CLAN OF GUINNESS WORLD RECORD HOLDERS, AS THEY MADE THE LONGEST *TORRONE* IN THE WORLD – A MERE 695 METRES LONG. THIS RECIPE MAKES A SHORTER BUT LOVELY SOFT *TORRONE*.

750g caster sugar

250ml honey

3 egg whites

125g icing sugar

400g almonds, roughly chopped

1 lemon, zest only

You will also need edible wafer paper, enough to line a 20cm x 20cm baking tin as well as a cover for the top

1 Lightly butter and line a 20cm x 20cm baking tin with edible wafer paper without overlapping the paper.

2 In a medium-sized pan, combine the sugar and honey over a medium heat. Cook until the temperature reaches hard crack stage (168°C) on a sugar thermometer. Remove from the heat and stir until the thermometer drops to soft crack stage (151°C).

3 In the meantime, beat the egg whites in a spotlessly clean, dry bowl until soft peaks form. Add the icing sugar and whisk again until stiff peaks form. With the mixer running, slowly pour the honey mix into the meringue. This will cause the meringue to double in size. Allow to stand until the volume returns to normal, then continue beating the mixture until it's thick. Fold in the almonds and lemon zest.

4 Pour the mixture into the lined baking tin. Cover with another layer of wafer paper and allow to cool.

5 Once cool, remove from the tin and cut into bite-sized pieces.

KEEPING IT LOCAL: BRITTAS BAY BRAMBLE HONEY GIVES THIS SPECIAL TREAT A RICH SMOOTHNESS AND A LOCAL TOUCH.

KEEPING IT LOCAL: BUY SOME PEARS FROM THE FARMERS' MARKET IN THE AUTUMN, THOUGH THEY MIGHT NEED TO BE POACHED FIRST TO SOFTEN THEM. ADD 1 PEELED, DICED PEAR TO THE CAKE MIXTURE FOR A LOVELY SMOOTH FLAVOUR. DECORATE THE TOP WITH SLICES OF POACHED PEARS.

PISTACHIO AND ORANGE CAKE

TORTA AL PISTACCHIO E ARANCIA / SERVES 8

I REMEMBER HAVING A DELICIOUS PISTACHIO CAKE IN VENICE YEARS AGO. I ACCIDENTALLY MENTIONED THIS AT A FAMILY GATHERING IN PALERMO JUST AS WE WERE UNWRAPPING THE BEAUTIFULLY PRESENTED SICILIAN PISTACHIO CAKE MADE WITH PISTACHIO NUTS FROM BRONTE BY THE FAMOUS LA PASTICCERIA CAPPELLO. A HUGE DEBATE AND A WONDERFULLY WARM CONVERSATION ENSUED, AND YES, BY THE END I TOO AGREED THAT THE SICILIAN VERSION IS BEST! THIS IS MY SIMPLIFIED VERSION OF THAT DELECTABLE CAKE.

160g pistachios, lightly toasted
220g butter, softened
200g caster sugar
3 eggs
1 orange, zest and juice
125g self-raising flour
1 tsp baking powder
3 tbsp milk, as required

FOR THE GLAZE:
150g caster sugar
1 orange, zest and juice
2 tbsp water
4 tbsp roughly chopped pistachios

1 orange, zest only, to decorate
natural yoghurt, to serve

1 Preheat the oven to 160°C/fan 140°C/gas 3. Lightly butter a 23cm springform cake tin and line the base with parchment paper.

2 Place the toasted pistachios into a food processor. Blend until smooth and set aside.

3 In a bowl, cream the butter and sugar together until pale and fluffy. Add the eggs one by one, followed by the orange zest and juice. Fold in the self-raising flour, baking powder and the ground pistachios. If the mixture is too stiff, add a little milk.

4 Pour the batter into the cake tin and spread the top evenly with a spatula. Bake for 30–35 minutes, or until an inserted skewer comes out clean. Leave in the tin for 5 minutes before transferring to a cooling rack.

5 In the meantime, to make the glaze, place the sugar, orange zest and juice and water in a small saucepan. Bring to the boil, reduce the heat and allow to simmer for 5–6 minutes, until the syrup thickens. Add the pistachios and simmer for 1 minute more. Remove from the heat and allow to cool.

6 Place the cake on a plate and drizzle the glaze over. Decorate with orange zest and serve with natural yoghurt.

WHITE CHOCOLATE AND WALNUT CREAM CUPS

COPPE DI CIOCCOLATO BIANCO E CREMA DI NOCI / MAKE 12 ESPRESSO CUPS

THESE LITTLE TREATS ARE SO ELEGANT FOR A WINTER EVENING DINNER PARTY. I MUST ADMIT THAT I HAVE A SLIGHT PASSION FOR PRETTY LITTLE ESPRESSO CUPS, SO I OFTEN TRAVEL HOME WITH A FEW BOXES OF LITTLE TREASURES IN MY SUITCASE!

550ml double cream
150g white chocolate drops
4 tbsp caster sugar
4 egg yolks
2 tbsp nocino (see page 198)

FOR THE CARAMELISED WALNUTS:
12 walnut halves, roughly chopped
200g caster sugar

1 Preheat the oven to 160°C/fan 140°C/gas 3. Butter 12 espresso cups.
2 Heat the cream until just boiling, then remove from the heat and add the chocolate and sugar. Whisk until the chocolate has melted. Add the egg yolks one by one and whisk quickly, ensuring all the yolks are incorporated. Stir in the nocino.
3 Pour this custard into the espresso cups and place them in a roasting tin. Pour hot water around the cups until it comes halfway up the side of the cups to act as a bain marie. Place in the oven and bake for 15–18 minutes, depending on the size of the espresso cups, until just set. There should still be a little wobble in the centre.
4 Remove the cups from the oven and allow to cool, then chill in the fridge for at least 6 hours or overnight.
5 Meanwhile, to make the caramelised walnuts, place a sheet of buttered parchment paper on a baking tray and scatter with the walnuts. Heat the sugar in a heavy-based pan until it's a rich golden colour. Take the pan off the heat immediately and pour the melted sugar over the walnuts. Allow to cool and set, then roughly chop the walnut brittle.
6 When you're ready to serve, decorate each cup with some caramelised walnuts.

KEEPING IT LOCAL: USE GLENILEN FARM DOUBLE CREAM FROM COUNTY CORK. WHEN MY HENS ARE ON STRIKE, I LIKE TO USE EGGS FROM THE NEIGHBOURING CROCKER'S ORGANIC FARM.

DRINKS

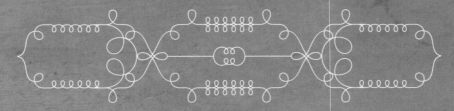

FROM COFFEES TO TISANES, *APERITIVI* TO *DIGESTIVE* AND *SPUMANTI* TO *VINI*, THE VARIETY, COLOUR AND FLAVOURS OF DRINKS IN ITALY ARE INTOXICATING. FRANGELICO, AMARETTO AND LIMONCELLO ARE FAVOURITES, BUT THERE ARE LOTS OF REGIONAL SECRETS, SUCH AS *LIQORE DI GELSI NERI*, A FRUITY MULBERRY LIQUEUR FROM SICILY.

BICERIN FROM TURIN, ORIGINALLY FROM THE CAFFÈ AL BICERIN, WAS SIPPED BY THE NOBLE LADIES WHILE THEY WAITED FOR THE LOCAL *INTELLIGENZIA* TO END THEIR DEBATES. THE LADIES HAD THE RIGHT IDEA – THIS DRINK IS A HEAVENLY LAYER OF RICH HOT CHOCOLATE FOLLOWED BY ESPRESSO AND FROTHED MILK OR CREAM ON TOP.

IN ROME, FENNEL TEA IS OFFERED AT THE END OF A MEAL. WELL KNOWN TO THE ANCIENT GREEKS, FENNEL TEA WAS LATER DISTRIBUTED AROUND EUROPE BY IMPERIAL ROME. IT NOT ONLY SETTLES THE TUMMY, BUT APPARENTLY IT ALSO IMPROVES EYESIGHT.

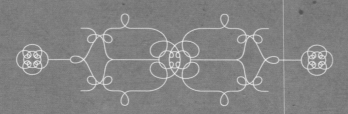

COFFEE

- ESPRESSO is in fact a *caffè* in Italy. (Espresso is the fast train!)

- AMERICANO is *caffè* with added water.

- MACCHIATO is *caffè* with a dash of milk, which can be hot or cold.

- CAPPUCCINO is *caffè* with frothed milk, usually enjoyed for breakfast and never after noon. The milk is apparently digested first, which gives energy, then the caffeine kicks in to keep you going.

- LATTE MACCHIATO is hot milk and a dash of *caffè*.

- MAROCCHINO is chocolate, *caffè* and hot milk.

- CAFFÈ CORRETTO is 'corrected coffee' – *caffè* with a liqueur added.

Coffee is enjoyed at home, in bars and restaurants, but never as a takeaway. In short, most Italians keep it simple: cappuccino for breakfast and *caffè* thereafter.

Sant'Eustachio is a famous coffee bar in Rome. Since it was featured in the *New York Times* the queues have been out the door, but it's still a favourite haunt of the locals. Interestingly, the role of the barista is not only to make the best coffee in the world, but to shield anyone from seeing how he makes it. Local legend has it that they add a pinch of flour to the coffee in order to get the creamy top that it's famous for, but I don't know because I couldn't see!

Here's how I make my *caffè* using a moka. A moka is a pot that produces coffee by passing hot water, pressurised by steam, through the ground coffee.

1 Rinse the inside of the base well, then fill with cold water to the point of the relief valve on the side.
2 Place the strainer onto the base and fill with espresso ground coffee, taking care not to pack the coffee in, otherwise the water won't be able to pass through.
3 Screw the top on reasonably tightly. Place on a low heat on the hob and wait for the magic.
4 After about 5 minutes, the upper cavity fills with this liquid gold and the aroma that fills the kitchen is intoxicating.
5 Pour into little cups, add sugar to taste and sip. For a creamy top, pour the coffee into a jug, add sugar and whisk, then divide into cups.

GRAPEFRUIT AND VODKA COCKTAIL

COCKTAIL DI POMPELMO E VODKA / SERVES 2

CLAUDIO'S COUSINS MADE THIS FOR ME ONE EVENING IN PALERMO AS AN *APERITIVO*. I TOOK A HUGE LIKING TO IT AND EVEN WENT BACK FOR SECONDS, TO MY DETRIMENT. BE CAREFUL, IT'S RATHER STRONG! (SEE PICTURE ON P. 192.)

50ml vodka
6 ice cubes
160ml fresh grapefruit juice
2 mint sprigs

1 Pour the vodka over the ice in a elegant highball glass and add the grapefruit juice.
2 Add a sprig of mint to each glass and serve.

KEEPING IT LOCAL: FOR A SWEETER VERSION, SUBSTITUTE D.P. CONNOLLY & SONS' CLOUDY PINK LEMONADE FOR THE GRAPEFRUIT JUICE.

LAVENDER LEMONADE

LIMONATA AL GUSTO DI LAVANDA / SERVES 8

WHETHER YOU CHOOSE TO USE THE LEMONS FROM SICILY OR FROM THE AMALFI COAST, THIS DRINK IS VERY REFRESHING AND DEFINITELY QUENCHES THE THIRST ON A HOT SUMMER DAY. SOMETIMES I KEEP THIS IN THE FREEZER UNTIL IT'S A LITTLE SLUSHY AND THEN SERVE IT. IT'S MY WICKLOW VERSION OF *GRANITA*!

250g caster sugar
1.2 litres water
2 tsp lavender flowers, washed well, plus extra to decorate
250ml lemon juice
ice cubes

1 Place the sugar and water in a large saucepan. Bring to the boil, then reduce the heat and simmer to form a thin syrup.
2 Add the lavender, cover and remove from the heat. Allow the syrup to infuse for at least 2 hours.
3 Strain the syrup and add the lemon juice.
4 Fill each glass with ice cubes and a lavender flower. Pour in the lemonade and serve.

KEEPING IT LOCAL: IN THE SUMMER I ALSO USE ROSE PETALS OR GORSE FLOWERS INSTEAD OF LAVENDER, BUT DO REMEMBER TO WASH THEM WELL.

WALNUT LIQUEUR

NOCINO / MAKES ABOUT 1.5 LITRES

CLAUDIO'S FAMILY HAS CREATED A PASTIME OUT OF MAKING HOMEMADE LIQUEURS - EVERYTHING FROM THE SICILIAN VERSION OF IRISH CREAM LIQUEUR TO A DELICIOUS MULBERRY LIQUEUR — BUT THE ONE THAT HAS INSPIRED ME THE MOST IS THEIR HOMEMADE NOCINO. I'M FORTUNATE ENOUGH TO HAVE TWO VERY OLD WALNUT TREES ON OUR FARM, BOTH OF WHICH PRODUCE LOTS OF GREEN WALNUTS BUT NOTHING USEFUL - UNTIL NOW! THE POOR SQUIRRELS ON THE FRONT LAWN WILL BE DEVASTATED AS I HARVEST THEIR SUPPER.

25 green walnuts, early enough in the season so that they are easily cut with a knife
500g caster sugar
1 litre grappa or vodka (highest-proof vodka available)
5 whole cloves
2 cinnamon sticks
zest of 1 lemon, cut into strips using a vegetable peeler
2 tsp vanilla extract

1 Rinse the walnuts and pat them dry. Cut them into quarters with a sharp knife. Be careful as you're cutting them – if you've waited too late in the season to pick them, their shells may have begun to harden.
2 Place the walnuts, sugar, grappa or vodka, cloves, cinnamon sticks, lemon zest and vanilla into a large glass container. The grappa or vodka must cover the walnuts. Shake well and place in a sunny spot for at least 6 weeks, shaking frequently to mix all the ingredients.
3 Remove the nuts and spices with a slotted spoon. Be careful, as the nocino stains. Strain the rest of the liqueur through a sieve into glass bottles. Secure with a tight-fitting lid and store in a cool, dark place.

KEEPING IT LOCAL: THE WALNUTS ARE TRADTIONALLY COLLECTED ON 24 JUNE, THE CELEBRATION OF THE FEAST OF SAN GIOVANNI, SO I SHALL BE HARVESTING LOCALLY THAT DAY.

MY FAVOURITE ITALIAN WINES

Isn't it refreshing to see 'wine in moderation' as part of the Mediterranean diet food pyramid? Wine simply completes a meal – it enhances the flavours and the ambience.

What I admire about Italian wines is the regional variety – the localisation of grapes which give each area its own unique wines. We're all familiar with the main grape varieties, such as Merlot and Chardonnay, and lovely they are too, but Italian wines bring intrigue to the table with their own special grape varieties and combinations.

ROSSO

MERIDIA IGT NERO D'AVOLA

I'm very fond of (and sentimentally attached to) this wine made from Sicily's local grape variety. The wines are charming and very easygoing, full of plummy fruit and spice with smooth, sweet tannins. Because these wines are still up and coming on the international markets, they are exceptional value and well worth seeking out. This wine works really well with pork chops and barbecued meats.

BORGO CIPRESSI CHIANTI

This world-famous wine comes from Tuscany, the heartland of fine Italian wine, and the grape variety here is called Sangiovese. Chianti comes in various guises and styles. I'd also recommend you try Chianti Rufina from the hills to the north of Florence or Chianti Classico from the 'classic' rolling vineyards between Sienna and Florence. This is the perfect wine for pasta and tomato-based sauces if you ask me!

ZENATO VALPOLICELLA SUPERIORE

Another great Italian dinner wine, I reckon that nowadays Valpolicella is giving Chianti a good run for its money in terms of popularity and quality. Made from three local grape varieties in the Veneto region, this is pretty much the house red wine in Venice and Verona. Keep an eye out for wines labelled as 'Superiore', as they're generally a good step up in quality. A great wine for risotto dishes.

MASI AMARONE CLASSICO

The 'big daddy' of all Italian reds in my view is the amazing Amarone. The wine is made using a very specific process of drying the grapes before fermentation, resulting in hugely concentrated aromas and flavours. The wine literally goes on and on and on. This wine is often called a *vino da meditazione*, or 'meditation wine', as it's one to sit back with, relax with and linger over its many gorgeous layers of character. A wonderful wine to try with Parmigiano and warm, crusty bread.

BIANCO

SAN GIORGIO PROSECCO 'FRIZZANTE'

It's amazing to see how popular Prosecco has become. It seems like just a few years ago no one had even heard of it! I guess part of the reason why it's so popular is that it's so dangerously easy to drink. It's also relatively inexpensive compared to Champagne and other sparkling wines (especially in the 'Frizzante' style). It's a great wine to welcome your guests with and to kick off a dinner party in style! It's also a lovely drink served with strawberries and cream.

ZENATO LUGANA 'SAN BENEDETTO'

One of my all-time favourite whites from the southern shores of Lago di Garda. It often has a beautiful apricot or peach fruit character, which I'm very fond of. Lugana is great with roast chicken and pasta dishes with a creamy sauce, like carbonara.

PIEROPAN SOAVE

This wine comes from vineyards in the Veneto region in and around the romantic town of Verona, home to Romeo and Juliet and world famous for opera. It's made from the wonderfully named Garganega grape and is one of Italy's most popular whites. Try a wine from a good producer, you won't be disappointed! Superb with monkfish or sea bass.

ARAGOSTA VERMENTINO DI SARDEGNA

A lovely dry, crisp white from Sardinia (which is nearly as beautiful an island as Sicily!). When I sit down to enjoy a well-chilled glass of Vermentino, I just know I'm going to taste bottled sunshine. This works particularly well with fish and seafood dishes, especially mussels and seafood risotto.

KEEPING IT LOCAL: FILL YOUR SUITCASE WITH THESE WONDERFUL WINES WHEN YOU'RE ABROAD, BUT WHEN BACK HOME, THERE IS NO SHORTAGE OF ITALIAN WINES. FOR ADVICE ON THE BEST, TRY JOHNNY MCGRATH OF NECTAR WINES IN SANDYFORD, DUBLIN, WHO IS ALWAYS ON HAND TO IMPART HIS EXPERTISE.

INDEX

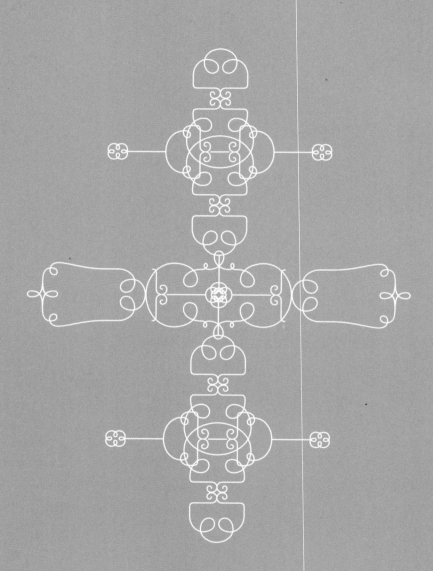